Moments on a Staircase

"Don't be satisfied with stories,

how things have gone with others.

Unfold your own story."

~ Rumi

Moments on a Staircase

Also by Mary Haylock

9249* (Silver Bow Publishing) 2019

Moments on a Staircase

by

Mary Haylock

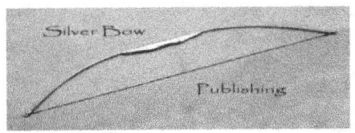

720 Sixth Street, Unit # 5
New Westminster, BC V3L 3C5
CANADA

Moments on a Staircase

Title: MOMENTS ON A STAIRCASE
Author: Mary Haylock
Cover Art: "Steps to Enlightenment" painting by Candice James
Layout and Design: Candice James
Editing: David Hardin

All rights reserved including the right to reproduce or translate this book or any portions thereof, in any form without the permission of the publisher. Except for the use of short passages for review purposes, no part of this book may be reproduced, in part or in whole, or transmitted in any form or by any means, electronically or mechanically, including photocopying, recording, or any information or storage retrieval system without prior permission in writing from the publisher or a license from the Canadian Copyright Collective Agency (Access Copyright). Copyright to all individual poems remains with the author.

ISBN 9781774030837 (softcover)
ISBN 9781774030844 (e-book)
© 2020 Silver Bow Publishing

Library and Archives Canada Cataloguing in Publication

Title: Moments on a staircase / by Mary Haylock.
Names: Haylock, Mary, 1939- author.
Identifiers: Canadiana (print) 2020019903X | Canadiana (ebook) 20200199765 | ISBN 9781774030837
    (softcover) | ISBN 9781774030844 (HTML)
Subjects: LCSH: Haylock, Mary, 1939- | LCSH: Haylock, Mary, 1939—Family. | LCSH: Authors, Canadian—
    Biography.
Classification: LCC PS8615.A845 Z46 2020 | DDC C818/.603—dc23

Table of Contents

Chapter 1:
    A Burns Baby: The fortuitous circumstances of my birth
Chapter 2:
    My Donnie Loved Me: A memorial to my brother Don
Chapter 3.
    Grandma: An amazing woman
Chapter 4:
    The Baby: My sister's traumatic arrival late in my life
Chapter 5:
    My Theatrical Career/How I fell in love with Leslie Howard
Chapter 6
    My Brief Affair with Dimitri Metropolis.
Chapter 7:
    Paul Suits Blue: In 1958 I married the love of my life
Chapter 8:
    The Happiest Day of my Life (Part 1):   Teddy is born
Chapter 9:
    The Happiest Day of my Life (Part 2): Jaime is born
Chapter 10:
    The Halls of Academia: By the grace of God I graduate
Chapter 11:
    The Equestrienne: Up, down, oomph!
Chapter 12:
    Beware of Greeks   Channelling Helen of Troy at sixty-two
Chapter 13
    The Scout: I am alone again
Chapter 14
    Old Men Need Not Apply.   Internet dating at seventy
Chapter 15:
    My Porkchop: I am knocked off my rocker
Chapter 16:
    A Christmas Letter: Ghosts of Christmas past

Chapter 17

Moments on a Staircase

Better Late than Never: At eighty I win an award
Chapter 18.
The End: I dreamed I went to Manderley again
Epilogue:
Nothing Lasts Forever: An imaginary ending to an unlikely affair

Prologue

When I was young, I helped my mother dust the old oak table in our dining room. My job was to get down on the floor and manoeuvre the oily cloth in and out of the intricate pattern carved into the heavy wooden pedestal. This was a ritual my mother and I carried out about four times a year when it was her turn to host her bridge club girls. I doubt they ever saw the result of my work, unless perhaps one of them dropped something on the floor and had to get down on her hands and knees to retrieve it. It was in case of this unlikely event that my mother insisted I get into all the nooks and crannies and use some elbow grease.

While I was working down below, mother would take her precious cups and saucers out of the china cabinet and lay them on top of the table. She matched each cup with its own saucer, and then spent some time deciding which eight cups she would use on this particular day, arranging and rearranging them in pretty little squadrons until they were just right. Then she'd find the plates and serving dishes she wanted to use and carry them into the kitchen to be washed. Everything looked pretty clean to me, but at nine-years-old, what did I know.

I would protest loudly at having to help with the housework. I hated it. But when it was time to dust the nether regions of the dining room table I didn't object.

That was because of the stories mother would tell me. Somehow, the opening of that china cabinet door was like revealing a portal to other times for her. She shared her "olden day" stories with me as I lay on the rug beneath the table.

"This cup with the violets belonged to Aunt Bella," she'd say, holding it down below the edge of the table so I could see. "Aunt Bella loved violets. She used to serve me hot chocolate from this cup. She was the one in the family with taste. She liked the finer things of life. She married a dentist from Beamsville who had lots of money."

I think mother liked the finer things of life, too, but instead of a dentist, she married a tire builder who worked at Firestone. Nevertheless, she seemed to feel a special kinship with this mysterious old aunt of hers who died long before I was born.

"Oh, look at this," she'd say. "It's a peach pit carved to look like the head of a horse. Uncle Ham made this. He'd carve all kinds of things out of dried peach pits and he used to give them to us kids. He and Aunt Luella never had children of their own."

I remembered them. He was a shy man with a thin moustache, and she was a pretty, gray-haired lady who always made me sit on her knee so she could kiss my cheek. I didn't mind because she smelled good and wore dangly earrings.

Then I'd hear a soft tinkle. "This is my favourite," mother would say. "Your father gave me this little glass bell on a very special occasion." Her voice would drift off into silence. She didn't have to show me the bell. I'd seen it many times before.

"What was the occasion?" I'd pipe up from down below.

"Maybe when you're all grown up, I'll tell you," was the familiar answer.

Then in a dreamy voice she'd say, "You know, Mary, your life is made up of special moments that you will always remember. Some of them are good and some not so good, but they are things you will never forget. I call them, *moments on a staircase*. Mother had a flair for the dramatic. She was a big fan of *Gone with the Wind*. These are some of my *moments on a staircase*.

Moments on a Staircase

Moments on a Staircase

Chapter 1 - A Burns Baby

I came into this world in the middle of a snowstorm. How Canadian can you get, eh?

It was the infamous, big blow of the winter of 1939. Of course, I don't remember it. But I've heard the story so many times that it must be somewhat true. At least I like to think so.

My mother began to notice my urgent desire to come out into the world shortly after midnight on the morning of the twenty-fifth of January. She waited politely until four in the morning so as not to disturb my father. He had been working afternoons building giant tires at the Firestone Tire and Rubber Company in Hamilton, and he needed his sleep. Outside, the wind was howling and snow was blowing sideways, straight across the windows, obscuring the streetlights and piling up against the doorways. A real nor'easter.

By the time mother got around to letting dad know what was happening, the snow had accumulated to a depth of two feet, and the roads were almost impassable. Dad started shovelling the driveway in a fury, horrified at the notion he might be alone with my mother at this delicate time. Like a madman, he cleared the way to the street, just wide enough for a car. Unfortunately, he didn't have one. So Mom got on the phone to Uncle George, who lived nearby. He owned a Reo Flying Cloud of questionable vintage and reliability. It was a large, cumbersome sedan with soft, cloth seats and a habit of not starting. Finally, it arrived at our door with my Aunt Dodie in the back seat. Dad climbed into the back beside her and they put mom in the front beside the driver. Dad had the presence of mind to take the snow shovel with him.

They were lucky. A snow plow roared by just as they were ready to hit the road. Dad jumped out of the car and made a dent in the large mountain of snow left at the end of the driveway by the big blade as it passed by. Uncle George revved up the motor and the old Reo roared backward through the gap, hitting the cleared pavement, skewing sideways and eventually straightening up to lumber along behind the enormous snow machine. The roadway stayed clear behind the plough just long enough for the car to keep moving.

By now, mother was getting quite uncomfortable in the front seat.

"Can you speed up a little, George?" she spit out between gritted teeth.

"Not unless you want me to run into the rear end of that snowplough," said Uncle George, puffing anxiously on the end of his old stogie.

Aunt Rhoda looked at her watch and said, "Tell me when the next pain comes, Eva."

"Aaaaaarrrgghhh!" mother said.

"Five-oh-three," Aunt Rhoda reported calmly.

"Where is this snowplough going?" asked my father, peering through the icy windshield at the swirling snow.

"I think we're heading up the mountain," answered Uncle George. "The hospital's right at the top. We should end up somewhere near there."

"We'd better, and sooooooon," groaned mother.

"Five-oh-seven," said my aunt.

"Shut up," yelled mother.

"I think it might be time to bear down," Rhoda announced matter-of-factly. She leaned over from the back seat and began to push down on mother's shoulders.

"Stop that! What are you doing?" mother cried.

"I'm helping you bear down," said Rhoda, who had no children of her own.

"Well knock it off, you're killing me."

When we finally arrived at the hospital, Uncle George abandoned the car in a nearby snowbank and he and dad made a chair of their crossed arms for mother to sit on. They carried us into the hospital through the waist-high drifts, mother moaning and dad shouting for a doctor. Uncle George was puffing and Aunt Rhoda was running beside them, still timing the pains, and me, trying very hard to get out of there.

At precisely eight-fifteen on the morning of January twenty-fifth, I made my entrance. A girl! Eight pounds-four ounces. Black hair and blue eyes. A child of the storm.

The exact timing of this momentous event is of the utmost importance. A black-haired child, born in stormy weather, on the anniversary of the birth of the great poet Robbie Burns? For my superstitious clan of transplanted Scottish relatives, the signs were all there. Good luck in spades!

Moments on a Staircase

Over the years I was invited many times to be *first foot* in the door of a Scottish house on New Year's Day. But it wasn't until some sixty years after my auspicious beginning that I attended a Burn's supper. It is celebrated every year by Scots all over the world. And what a great excuse to get together in the dead of winter to eat and drink and chase away the bone-numbing cold. A special meal is served, complete with the haggis, a kind of oatmeal and tripe pudding laced with enough spices to give anyone heartburn for a week. No one eats it. At the party I attended, it was piped in by a member of the local police pipe band and set upon the table in a place of honour.

What followed was a feast like none other. Glasses were filled and raised and downed at every opportunity; a toast to the bard, a toast to all the ladies present and even a toast to the awful pudding itself. Because of the circumstances of my birth, I had been asked by my hostess to give the reply to the toast to the ladies, an honour indeed. After dinner I waited patiently for the other toasts to be pronounced. They were uniformly solemn and sincere and received with polite applause.

And then it was my turn. I rose from my chair and waited a moment for silence. When all eyes were upon me, I commenced speaking in the nearest thing to a Scottish accent I could muster:

> Thanks be for raisin' up yur glasses,
> To drink a toast to these fair lasses.
> These are gud words wi' which you praise us,
> So muckle much it doth amaze us!
>
> For 'tho we dressed oursel' full fancy,
> Wi' scarves and lace and shoes fair dancey,
> Trowelled make-up in our nooks and crannies
> So we'd naught look sae much like grannies,

Moments on a Staircase

And tho our eyes be fu' o twinkles
We hard-pressed be to hide our wrinkles!
But you ha'e wooed our semple hearts
And made us feel like toothsome tarts.

For this--full thanks! But be ye wary
If thinkst thou wi' us ye'll tarry.
If ye be plottin' how ye'll shag us
Ye'll find yer balls in next year's haggis!

    I finished with a flourish and saw the faces of my fellow diners turned to look at me, their expressions aghast, mouths open. And then they started to laugh. They laughed until some of them fell out of their chairs and onto the floor. They were still laughing when they put on their boots and coats, their mittens and scarves, their ear muffs and nose warmers. Then they went out into the frigid air of that mid-winter night feeling, I think, a wee bit warmer inside. I like to think that Robbie Burns would have been laughing too.

Chapter 2 - My Donnie Loved Me

There has been one man in my life who was there from the day I was born until he left me after seventy-nine years. My brother, Donnie. I called him Donnie when we were young because that's what everyone called him back then. And I continued to call him Donnie all his life, even after everyone else called him Don or Dammie, Dad or Papa Donnie or Uncle Don. He was always Donnie to me. And not only Donnie, but MY Donnie!

My first memory of My Donnie was an incident that happened when I was just a year old. I think I remember, but probably it was listening to the story Mom told me when I was older that made me think so. I'm not sure. Donnie would have been sixish. Much too big to play in a playpen. But that was the only place in the house where I couldn't get at him. He would climb into my playpen with his long, gangly legs so that he could play with his cars and trucks in peace. Mom put me on the floor outside the playpen looking in. I could climb out by myself, but couldn't climb in. One day when Donnie ventured out of this safe environment for a few minutes, I bit him on the arm. I had some new teeth and wanted to try them out, I guess. I bit him hard and made him cry. So, Mother applied the remedy for this behaviour that was popular at the time. She bit me back!

Moments on a Staircase

The thought was, this would teach me how it felt to bite someone and I wouldn't do it any more.

I suppose it was a plausible theory, but in my two-year-old mind, I was horrified that my usually loving and gentle mother had inflicted a lot of pain on my chubby little arm. Any connection to what I had done was unfortunately lost on me.

The irony of what happened next tells a lot about My Donnie's loving nature, even at this young age. I burst into indignant tears and ran over to where he sat on the rug nursing his sore arm. He immediately opened his arms to enclose me in a warm hug.

"Donnie! Mommy *bited* me," I wailed.

He patted my back and kissed my tear-stained cheek.

"But darling," he said. "You bit Donnie. You mustn't bite people. It's not nice."

What six-year-old boy would react this way? Not too many, I think. But that was My Donnie. He picked me up and put me into the playpen. Then he climbed in with me and let me play with his toys, safe from any further vicious attacks from our mother.

I think I remember the feeling of warmth and comfort that filled my heart with love for him at that moment. He was my hero and my buffer against the harshness of life for the rest of his life.

I always knew that, no matter what I did, My Donnie loved me.

He proved it again and again in many ways over the years. I remember an infamous day when I got the strap in grade two. I had finished my work and instead of sitting quietly with my hands behind my back until all the other children were done, as we were supposed to do, I snuck a red crayon out of my desk and made a small picture of a flower on the inside cover of my workbook. Miss Calder caught me and put my name on the blackboard, right under Joe Seath's name. Joe got the strap every day for some offence or other. At the end of the day, before class was dismissed, we got to witness Joe howling and yowling as the strap descended time and again on his skinny outstretched hand. The rest of us giggled behind our hands at his antics.

But now, I was in the lineup to get the strap. I finished out the day in a state of dread. Now I would be the one everyone was laughing at. The injustice of it all filled my six-year-old soul with outrage, but I was determined not to cry. Actually, I don't remember the physical pain, but I will never forget the embarrassment and horror I felt. I was one of the good kids. How could this be happening to me?

I held back the tears until I got outside on the playground and saw Donnie standing there with a group of his grade eight friends. I ran to him crying and told him of my disgrace at the hands of the evil Miss Calder.

He took me by the hand and we walked to the bike rack where he sat me on the seat of his bike and we pedalled off to pick up his newspapers. His route was Lake Avenue and we lived about halfway down the street. When we got to the first house, Donnie folded the paper and threw it up on the porch. As he did he yelled, "Miss Calder is a fat old cow!" I was amazed at this bad language coming from him, but secretly I was pleased.

At the next house, he handed me the paper and I tossed it up on the front porch.

"Miss Calder is a mean old witch!" I shouted at the top of my lungs.

And so we continued, coming up with a different, nasty slur for every porch. By the time we got to our house I was feeling much better and Donnie and I were laughing uproariously at our daring deed. He had to go on to finish his paper route and I skipped into the house to tell mom about my unfair treatment.

When I had finished mother said, "Did you know you weren't supposed to colour in your book?"

"Yes," I answered, sheepishly.

"Then I guess you should do what your teacher tells you to do, shouldn't you?"

"Yes mom."

"Go and wash your face and hands for supper," she said.

I went upstairs and didn't find out until I was a grown woman that my mother had called the school and complained to the principal about what she considered brutal treatment for such a minor offence. At supper that night, Donnie and I snickered every time our eyes met. We were the only ones who knew that we had evened the score with that wicked teacher.

No matter what I did, I knew that My Donnie loved me.

And so it continued for the rest of our days. In my life, a beloved husband and precious grandson, dear friends and relatives came and went. But always, always My Donnie was there for me.

Recently, at the age of eighty-two, he noticed that the stairs down to the lake at my cottage were too steep and precarious for me to navigate safely. Donnie decided we needed some kind of a hand rail. In his subtle way he suggested this to my two sons.

"Yes, definitely," they agreed. "We'll get right on it."

When they didn't do it soon enough for him, Donnie appeared at our dock one day with a boatload of tools and some metal pipes and fittings. Without any ado he set about to build the railing all by himself. The boys weren't around, but when they came back, there it was. A sturdy, if somewhat wonky-looking, iron railing extending to the dock.

My Donnie is gone now, but the railing is still there, firmly in place, keeping me safe. When I walk down the steps with my hand on that railing I can almost feel him holding my hand.

The only time he ever let me down was when he didn't keep his promise to write my eulogy when I died.

"Try to think of something good to say about me." I said.

"Don't worry, Mare, I'll just make something up."

There aren't too many sure things in this life, but one thing I know without a doubt. My Donnie loved me.

Chapter 3 - Grandma's House

The woman I most admired in my life was my grandma, Agnes House. I can picture her as if she were standing in front of me right now. At first glance, there is nothing really remarkable about her. She is a big-boned woman, tall and straight with her gray hair pulled back in a bun. Her face is weather beaten and expressionless, marked by a few shapeless brown blotches here and there, acquired by spending a lifetime working in the sun. Her mouth turns down naturally at the corners giving her a severe look. No make-up, not even a touch of lipstick to brighten things up. Just her eyes, twinkling behind her glasses, give a hint that she is perhaps more interesting than she appears. She wears a clean, print housedress with a full apron over top. Straps over the shoulders, tied in a flat bow at the back. No frills, nothing too colourful or fussy. Plain and utilitarian, as is her shape. Straight up and down, no softness or curves to indicate she is a woman. Her legs are shapely though, long and slim from ankle to knee.

"Best legs in the family," everyone agrees, even though no one has ever glimpsed anything above her knees. She usually wears light brown stockings rolled up under the hemline of her housedress. In summer, this changes to a pair of white ankle socks. But always the same sturdy, black lace-up Oxfords on her feet. Her ankles puff out over the tops like mushroom caps. This is how she looks at forty when I first knew her. And at fifty. By the time she is sixty, the hairstyle changes to a short, nondescript cut with a few curls, the white tinged with blue from a rinse at the hairdressers. Then seventy, eighty.

I have gone from a kid to a married woman with grown children. Her hair has a yellowish cast now, but she wears the same dress, the same apron, the same glasses, the same shoes. The familiar face looks just the same. How did she manage to stop the clock for so many years while I was growing older? I wish I knew. But what a comfort to know she was always there in her little white house on Twenty Highway, doing whatever it was she did all day and never changing year after year. A nondescript woman leading a nondescript life. Or so we thought.

But that's not exactly true. It's hard to believe the things she did in her lifetime. At the beginning of the century when she was a young married woman with three small children she homesteaded on the prairies with grandpa, when the west, according to the Canadian government, who was giving away large parcels of land, saying it was *the only place to be*. Many young farmers were lured out of Ontario to take advantage of this offer, and Agnes and Percy set out on a train for North Battleford, Saskatchewan with high hopes. They lived out on the plains in a 'soddy' made of dirt and grass and hunted for the meat they ate.

One day while hunting partridges, they left the children under a tree and walked the field some distance apart, hoping to flush out their dinner. A couple of birds would make a tasty meal later on. When she was quite a distance away, something caused Agnes to look back at the tree and what she saw made her freeze in her tracks. A ring of wolves was silently closing in on the babies playing in the shade. She screamed for Percy and they both ran at the pack, shouting and shooting their guns in the air. The noise scared off the wolves and they slunk away into the tall grass.

Later, when grandma told the story, she pointed out that if she hadn't felt compelled to look back, none of us grandchildren would be here today. Somehow, she made it seem like some divine intervention had saved us. Left unspoken was the impression that we had better live up to the expectations of our rescuer.

When the Great Drought drove them off the prairie, grandma and grandpa gave up their western dream and came back east to Stoney Creek. The family farm had been divided up among grandpa's half-brothers while he was away out west, and there was nothing left of it for him. He and grandma lived in the city for a while and grandpa worked for the Hamilton Street Railway, the HSR. After their kids grew up and moved away, he and grandma rented a few acres of land on Highway Twenty near Number Eight Highway.

The road was so quiet back then, I often rode the plough horse, Queenie, to visit my friend Marlene on the other side of the highway. No saddle, no bridle, just hanging on with my legs and the occasional gee or haw.

On grandpa's property stood a little white clapboard cottage, an outhouse, a large wooden barn and some very nice soil which grandpa described as "just like brown sugar".

He became a market gardener and grandma helped him. They grew tomatoes and beans, beets and asparagus and radishes. There were straw-covered rows of berries, a few rows of raspberry bushes and at the end of the rows, some red and black currents and a couple of gooseberry bushes. Grandpa was a good farmer. The plants grew tall and green and Queenie and grandpa ploughed between the rows to keep the weeds out. Queenie placed her dainty old racehorse feet carefully so she didn't damage the plants and grandpa walked behind hanging onto the handles of the plough, reins around his neck, talking to her to let her know what he wanted her to do.

"Haw, now, Queen. Come on girl. Round we go. Gee, gee there. Whoa, girl." I think she could have done it on her own, though. She knew the routine so well.

Grandma looked after the kids Grandpa picked up in Hamilton early on summer mornings to come and harvest the fruit and vegetables. He'd stop at Parkdale and Normanhurst, a couple of the less affluent neighbourhoods in Hamilton, and load up the back of his old red truck with a scruffy array of pickers. When they got to the farm, grandma would assign them their rows and get them started in the field. She kept track of their names and how many baskets they picked on a slat from one of the crates that held the strawberries for market. She also noticed who didn't have enough lunch in his bag or who needed a pat on the back or a shoulder to cry on. At the end of the day, grandma stood at the back of the truck and called out the names and how much they had earned and grandpa paid them out of his pocket. The two Peace sisters always made the most.

"Bev Peace," grandma would say, "three dollars."

"Mary Peace, two-fifty."

I, on the other hand, was practically useless. It must have been embarrassing for grandma to call out my pay.

"Mary Gillies, fifty-cents." At five-cents a quart, that didn't amount to much of a day's work. And truthfully, grandma used to come and help me fill up my baskets when I got hot and tired and wanted to quit. I preferred to make fairies from the colourful hollyhock blossoms that grew near the outhouse, which I visited frequently during the day, hoping no one noticed my absence from the fields. While I was gone, a couple of my baskets would miraculously fill themselves.

I also enjoyed the privilege of eating lunch with grandma in her kitchen. Just before twelve o'clock, she would leave the fields and head for the house with her arms full of whatever was being picked, yellow beans or asparagus or beets. That's how we knew what would be for lunch that day. Lunch was really more like dinner. After dinner, grandpa would have a nap on the settee in the living room. He always fell asleep with a cigarette in his mouth and the long, curved ash hung precariously on the end of it until grandma came along and yelled at him, "Percé, watch your ash!"

Early on Saturday morning in the summer, around five o'clock, grandpa would load up the truck and head for the market in downtown Hamilton. He had a stall there where he set up a long table near the tail end of the truck and hung his sign, "Perc House, Grower". Sometimes grandma went with him to help sell the beautiful fruits and vegetables to the rich city women who came with their maids carrying baskets to buy fresh produce. Grandpa kept special goodies under the counter for them, like the tiny little new potatoes he wasn't supposed to sell for anything but pig fodder.

Once in a while, grandma took me to market with her and I helped sell stuff. I learned to make change from the old cigar box under the table. Usually, she and I went out to the Majestic restaurant for lunch. I don't think I had ever been to a restaurant before I went with her. I could order whatever I wanted from the menu. After lunch it was a big treat to go to the Cut-Rate shoe store upstairs and look at the bones in my feet in the x-ray machine. If it had been a really good morning at the market, grandma sometimes tried to buy me a new pair of shoes or a pretty dress at Eaton's. But I didn't like to try things on, and I was cranky and stubborn. One day, when I was particularly obnoxious, grandma told my mother when we got home that she would never take me shopping again, and she never did.

A long time after she was gone, I saw her account book for this little farming operation they lived on. She kept careful track in a scribbler with lines she had drawn at one side of the page. One box for what they brought in from the sale of their produce, the others for what it cost them. Rent for the little property, heat, light, seeds from Tregunno's, salaries for Jerry Peace, the hired man, and Old Mary, grandpa's second in command. She spoke little English and only grandpa could understand her, but she was born bent over with a hoe in her hand and a black kerchief around her hair. It makes me laugh now to realize that Old Mary was probably about thirty-five. After all the expenses, and all their work, they cleared twenty-three dollars. That had to last them for the whole month. And by some miracle, it did. And out of this pittance she wanted to buy me a new dress.

I don't imagine they could have survived if grandma hadn't preserved so much of what they grew in jars and bottles down in the basement. There was always lots to eat at grandma's house. Jams and jellies, peaches and pears, pickled beets and relish and chili sauce. Every meal was enhanced by the wonderful contents of her preserving jars. And she was a good cook. Nothing fancy, just plain, tasty meals built around a cheap cut of meat done to tender perfection in her pressure cooker. Nobody could make beef brisket like grandma. And in summer, there would be yellow beans piled high on the plate with canned salmon, brown bread and for dessert, a dish of homemade fruit salad. Dinner always ended with something sweet. She would let us kids go down cellar and pick whatever we wanted from the shelves. A special treat to go with the fruit was grandma's cinnamon toast made with butter and brown sugar and cinnamon, spread thickly on a piece of bread. Once in a while, she served something exotic from the Mammy's bakery truck

Moments on a Staircase

that passed by every day, like Eccles cakes or a Spanish bar cake that she would hide behind the glass doors of her pantry until dinner time. When dinner was over, she did the dishes at the big sink by the window, where the red Lifebuoy soap sat in its little wire holder covered in pink bubbles from grandpa's washing up. I don't ever remember helping grandma with the dishes.

Sometimes, after he finished his tea, grandpa would tease me. He kept his razor strop hanging near the washing machine in the kitchen so he could sharpen his straight razor before he shaved at the sink in the morning. He would chase me around with the strop, stamping his feet and pretending he was going to spank me with it. How I hated this little game! Grandma would come and stand between us with her hands on her hips, facing him down.

"Percé, stop it," she would say. "She doesn't like it."

I felt safe when she was around. Not too sure about him, but always knowing she would be on my side and protect me.

Grandma and grandpa never had a soft word for each other, at least not that I heard. Something had happened to their relationship over the years. Maybe it was the death of their western dream or maybe his drinking before he went to Toronto for the *'gold cure'*. Or perhaps it was just the harshness of life, having to scrape away to make a living, I don't suppose we will ever know. Grandma certainly didn't talk about it. But she had a particular disgusted tone of voice on those rare occasions when she spoke to him. And he would glare at her and say that the next time he got married it would be to an Indian squaw who knew her place. For all the time I knew them, they slept in separate bedrooms.

At Christmas time, when my brother Don and I snuck downstairs in our house on Lake Avenue, I would sit for a few minutes on the stairs, looking through the railing into the living room, savouring the excitement at what I saw waiting by my stocking in the half-light of early morning. There would always be a new doll. And it never occurred to me to be surprised when the dress it wore was made of the same material as grandma's latest apron. One year the doll was in a beautiful bassinet with a skirt of white-dotted swiss, starched to perfection, ruffles gathered all around the edge and finished with a beautiful satin bow at each corner of the hood. It was the same dotted swiss that was in the old curtains grandma had just taken down from her bedroom window. And the little quilt in the doll's bed contained smaller patches of the same material as the large quilt stretched on the rack in grandma's living room, waiting for her church group to come and help her stitch it together. I never thanked her, of course, since these were Santa gifts, and I didn't make the connection at all in my avaricious little brain. Grandma just sat and smiled when she came over for dinner later in the day and I showed her each one of these things Santa had brought me. She admired them as if she had never seen them before, without giving me a clue about their origins.

"Yas, yas," she would say, smiling fondly at me.

She was constant and unchanging for most of my life. One year, mom and dad had an accident on New Year's Eve. They were involved in a collision with a drunk driver, and when I woke up in the night, grandma was there. When mother got sick and went away, grandma came to look after us and she took the baby, Barbara, to her house and cared for her while mother was ill.

Agnes lived in her little house with grandpa for many years and for all those years, she was always the same. And then, after grandpa died at eighty-six, something unheard of happened. She packed her bags and took a train to New York City. As far as I know, she had not been anywhere since she and grandpa went to Florida to visit Uncle Stan and Aunt Elsie in their trailer many years ago. The whole family was dumbfounded. Where had she gone, and why?

Then the pieces of the puzzle began to fall into place. For many years she had corresponded with a former teacher at Red Hill School. His name was Harry Hooker. He later left teaching and became a doctor. His last job was as resident doctor of the Waldorf Astoria. He lived in the penthouse and received what I imagine would have been a substantial salary. He also bought I.B.M. stock when it was first issued, and this alone would have made him a rich man. Harry had married after he left teaching and once, he and his wife came to visit grandma and grandpa. I remember being introduced to them and thinking how stylish and well-to-do they looked.

He was tall and distinguished and she wore beautiful clothes and a gorgeous hat with a veil. They looked out of place in grandma's little sitting room with one of Dr. Hooker's shiny shoes covering the burn on the rug from grandpa's cigarette. Grandma served them tea in her best china cups.

After his wife died, grandma continued to correspond with Dr. Hooker. His letters were works of art, written in elegant flourishes with a black pen. I think he was grandma's intellectual guru in life. He would discuss books he had read and politics and philosophy and poetry with her and this must have satisfied a latent hunger in grandma for knowledge of the world beyond her secluded life on the little five-acre farm. She saved all Harry Hooker's letters tied with a blue ribbon in a cedar-lined box on her dresser and I read them after she died. It was interesting to see how they progressed from purely academic discussions of the news of the day at first, to more intimate revelations of their innermost feelings and thoughts, later on. I think they fell in love during their years of correspondence and his letters that in the beginning had ended, "Sincerely, Harry Hooker", in the last stages of their long distance romance finished with a heartfelt, "Ever Yours, Hook".

Grandma didn't tell anyone she was going to visit him. Her husband had just died, and she was in her eighties. Mother would certainly have tried to talk her out of it. It was a rash and crazy thing to do.

But grandma got on a train all by herself and went to New York City and she had a wonderful time. After all, this was a woman who had homesteaded on the prairie in a covered wagon, so what did she have to fear?

Hook was on his deathbed, confined to his room and cared for by a housekeeper. He was in his nineties. While grandma was there, she went shopping on Fifth Avenue, driven by Hook's chauffeur. He took her from store to store and carried her parcels for her just like the rich New York city matrons. I don't know what she bought. Nothing frivolous, I expect.

Before she left, Harry asked her to stay with him and be his companion. He didn't want her to be poor anymore. The housekeeper would look after the house, he said. He just wanted her there with him for a little while before he died to keep him company. She said no.

Before she left New York, he tried to give her some money, but she refused that offer too. She just wasn't that kind of girl. He begged her to take some little memento with her to remind her of him when she was back at home. He must have known he would never see her again. She took a candy dish, a milk glass hen sitting on a nest, from the china cabinet in the dining room. They said their goodbyes and grandma headed back to her real life. Hook died shortly after.

Moments on a Staircase

In the *Hamilton Spectator*, it was announced that he had made a bequest of twenty-five million dollars to his old alma mater, McMaster University. When we grandchildren found out how wealthy he was we said, "Grandma, why didn't you take a million or two when he asked you?"

"Certainly not," she replied. "What would I do with all that money?"

"But Grandma," we whined in unison, "You could have given it to us, your poor grandchildren."

"Earn it yourselves," was her stern reply.

Moments on a Staircase

Chapter 4 - The Baby

In 1950 we were a nice little family, mother, dad, Donnie and I, living happily in our new house on Lake Avenue Drive in Stoney Creek. At the supper table one night, mom and dad smiled mysteriously at each other and asked us how we would feel about having a baby brother or sister. Donnie said, "Yes," immediately. At sixteen, what did he care? He'd soon be out of there on his way to university.

I, on the other hand, was only eleven. Even at that young age, I sensed this could have a significant impact on my life. I thought about it for a minute or two, then I said, "Okay, but only if it's a girl." I had no idea this was something my parents had no control over.

Things went on as usual, except that mother grew larger before our eyes. And I could hardly wait until my little sister would magically appear. I would lie on the couch in the living room, gazing out at the catalpa trees and counting the days until August when I would have a sister of my very own. I would look after her, of course, and take her for rides in her buggy. She would sleep in the crib dad put up in my room and follow me everywhere and love only me, just like the puppy my mom wouldn't let me have

Moments on a Staircase

because she was afraid of dogs. I would call her Lulu and teach her to walk and talk and do other tricks. I could hardly wait.

A set of unfortunate circumstances caused my mother to go into labour early and dad whisked her off to the hospital on the night of June 23rd.

It was a wild, stormy night and the catalpa trees were outlined by flashes of lightning as I looked out my window, waiting anxiously for mom and dad to come back. Suddenly, it occurred to me that the baby sister they were bringing home might, by some quirk of fate, be a boy. We hadn't heard anything from the hospital yet, so I decided to find out for myself.

"If the lightning strikes twice, it's a girl," I intoned solemnly to the midnight sky.

With some kind of superstitious serendipity, the next clap of thunder announced a double whammy of lightning. Two super kilowatt flashes, one after the other. It's a girl! I went happily to bed and found out in the morning that I was right.

But everything wasn't alright. The baby couldn't come home because she weighed only four pounds-four ounces. They had to keep her in the hospital in an incubator. After a week, mom and dad came home empty handed with worried looks on their faces. The talk was not about when she would come home, but if. I would have worried too, except that another thunderstorm came along and this time I posed the proposition--two strikes she lives. One, she dies. Once again, the thunder gods gave me the answer I wanted to hear. But mom and dad weren't convinced when I told them not to worry, the baby would soon come home to us.

And home she came a few weeks later, all five pounds of her, red-faced and squeaking in the little doll's bonnet mom had knitted while she was in the hospital. We took turns feeding her every couple of hours and it became a contest to see who could get her to drink the most from her bottle. Two ounces was a real feat. The trick was to keep her awake after the first couple of swigs.

I soon became the best at that, because when no one was looking I snapped the bottom of her feet with my fingers or pinched her cheeks just a little. Under my loving care she started to thrive. We even decided to give her a name, Barbara Elizabeth. But those of us who lived with her just called her "the baby".

She didn't like to sleep in her crib which was in my bedroom. We took turns rubbing her back and singing to her. When one of us had done our shift, someone else would come along to take over. Often, we would fall asleep ourselves, hanging over the bars of baby's crib. I got used to having an endless parade of people in my bedroom throughout the night. It took all of us and my grandmother to take care of the baby for the first few months of her life. Was it worth it? I began to have some doubts.

Mother suffered some health problems at this time and Don spent more and more time at his friend Barry's house where he could play the piano in peace without fear of waking up the baby. Dad worked shifts and I was the only one who was always hanging around, so it was me who often ended up looking after the baby. And there was always something wrong with her. When mom and dad came back from one of baby's frequent trips to the doctor, mom would often be in tears and dad would be gruff and upset. They would rush past me, thrust the little bundle of baby into my arms and go upstairs to their bedroom. I would unwrap her and wonder what was wrong with her now. I found out later.

She had colic. She was constipated. She had terminal diaper rash. It was always something that needed tending to. But somehow, she hung on with an amazing, stubborn tenacity for one so small and managed to grow up.

I taught the baby to walk to the best of my ability. She had cataracts in her eyes from the oxygen in the incubator, but we didn't know this until much later.

It would have explained her bumping into things and falling down a lot. Much of the time she rode around on my back as I galloped on my hands and knees through the house.

There was nothing wrong with her speech, however. She was smart as a whip and picked up easily on her first words--mommy, daddy, horsey ride--but I don't think she ever said Mary. We had a Mammy's baker who came to the door every day with his basket of goodies, horse and wagon standing out at the street. He was young and good looking. He seemed to like to chat with mom at the kitchen door.

She got red and flustered when we teased her about that. I thought it would be funny to teach the baby to say, "Mommy kissed the baker." One day when dad was having breakfast at the kitchen table, the baker came to the door. The baby smiled at him from her highchair and repeated what I had taught her. "Mommy kissed the baker," she piped up, clear as a bell. Needless to say, dad was not amused. The baker soon left this route for another one in Winona.

When she was three or four, the baby still had trouble sleeping. By now Don had gone off to university and my sister had his old room to herself, but sometimes she still didn't want to go to bed. I would lie down beside her and weave a magic tale of kings and queens and beautiful princesses who lived in a magnificent castle. Of course, she was the princess. I usually cast myself as the evil fairy godmother who tried to put a spell on her. Wishful thinking perhaps.

Moments on a Staircase

As the baby grew up, we did fewer things together. I had a job at the theatre in town and she had her own little group of friends and started school, where she excelled despite her difficulty seeing properly. It was Don's girlfriend, Mimi, who finally convinced mom and dad to take her to the eye doctor where she acquired a pair of thick glasses that helped her to see. She hated them. Maybe it helped that I wore glasses too, because she thought I was the most beautiful creature on earth. Once when I was getting ready for a blind date upstairs in my room, I heard a knock on the front door. I told the baby to go and answer the door while I finished dressing. Next thing I knew, the door to my room opened and standing there was the baby, with my date by the hand.

I was in my underwear, no make-up, hair all messed up. The poor guy didn't know where to look. "Here she is," gushed the baby. "Isn't she beautiful?" No wonder I never heard from him again.

On my wedding day a few years later, the baby stole the show. Most of my friends had to borrow somebody else's adorable, blonde, curly-headed angel for a flower girl; a friend's daughter, a second cousin twice removed. Not me. I had my very own little sister; knobby knees, poker straight brown braids, pop bottle glasses and all. But she suited me just fine. And she always will.

Moments on a Staircase

Chapter 5 - My Theatrical Career

I like to say that I went *into the theatre* in 1952 at the age of thirteen. It sounds so glamorous. But really, it was a street corner dare from a couple of girlfriends on our way home from high school that makes it happen. Everyday we pass the new building on King Street that is to house a real *bona fide* theatre in our little town, complete with marquis and flashing lights and a towering rectangular sign that reads *"Fox Theatre"* in letters a foot high. Everyone is filled with anticipation. Until now, we kids have shuffled into the Scout house every Saturday afternoon to sit on hard wooden benches and for a dime watch a couple of black and white movies flicker before our eyes. One is the feature, usually Charlie Chaplin sashaying around twirling his cane, or a terrified Harold Lloyd swinging from the hands of an enormous clock two stories up. It is most often a comedy and we kids laugh it up, not so much at what we see on the screen, but contagiously from the sound of the other kids laughing around us. After the intermission, things get serious. The second offering is always a cliff-hanger, where some wan heroine gets herself tied up to a railroad track and just as the train comes thundering into view, smoke bellowing from the engine, the screen freezes and flaming letters announce that we have to wait till next time to see what happens. This is greeted with a communal groan. But we always come back for more. It is, after all, the highlight of our week.

Now we wait anxiously for the new theatre to open, not knowing what to expect, but hopeful that it will be better than we are used to.

The Monday before the grand opening, I stand across the street from the new theatre with my two girlfriends, Nellie and Joan. We always hang around at that corner for a while after school because Joan goes home in a different direction. Nellie and I live on the same street, quite close to each other, so we go the other way together.

"I applied for a job in the new show," Nellie says. "The guy says he'll call me this week. I hope I get it." She tosses her yellow ringlets and smiles a sneaky little smile.

"I did too," says Joan. They look at each other for a minute, surprised. "There are quite a few jobs, like cashier and candy counter person and ushers," Joan continues. "Maybe we'll both get a job, Nellie. Johnny Armondo says he got a job as an usher because his dad knows the owner, Mr. Di Salvo."

"Yah. That'd be fun. Why don't you apply, Mary? Then we could all work together."

"I don't wanna." I say. I know I can't compete with them.

"Chicken!" They laugh with their heads together, already looking like a pair of special friends with a secret.

"Go on, Mary. There's the owner right there cleaning the front doors. Go on. I dare you. Just ask him for a job," says Nellie, pushing me toward the curb.

I stick my chin out and head across the street to where a dark-haired man is spraying blue liquid on one of the big front doors and rubbing it with a towel. *I'll show those two I'm not a chicken.* But my insides are fluttering against my ribs as I get closer to the man.

"Hi," I say. "Do you have any jobs?"

He stops rubbing and stares at me. Dark eyes narrow as he looks me up and down. There isn't much to see. I am tall and sturdy. At thirteen I have developed breasts that I really don't know what to do with, so I wear baggy sweaters to school and hope no one will notice. My skirt is navy and straight up and down with no shape to it at all. I made it in Home Economics. I got a *C minus*. My saddle shoes are scuffed and badly in need of some whitening. What am I doing? Joan and Nellie are little and cute and always look well put together. They are both cheerleaders. He wouldn't want me.

"Do you have a white blouse?" the man says.

"Yes."

"Wear it with that skirt and come early on Friday night. It's opening night, so come around five o'clock so I can show you what to do. Awright?"

"Okay." I walk in a daze back to the two on the corner who are waiting for me.

"Hey," the man shouts," what's your name?"

"Mary," I say.

"See you Friday, Mary."

By the time I reach them Nellie and Joan are staring at me open-mouthed.

"What happened?" says Nellie.

Moments on a Staircase

"I got a job." I say. And only then does it begin to sink in. I have trumped them at their own little teasing game of *dare ya*. I got the job.

"What are you going to do?" asks Joan.

"I dunno," I say. "All's I know is, I got a job in the theatre." Right then I fall in love with the sound of it. I can hardly wait to get home to tell my mom and dad.

I have a real job. Not baby sitting or picking berries at my grandfather's farm. A real job *in the theatre!* It is the beginning of what are to be some of the happiest days of my life.

Opening night at The Fox is a confusing blur. Outside the theatre several large posters advertise the movie, '*Wait till The Sun Shines, Nellie*', in glorious Technicolour. I find out from Mr. DiSalvo that I am to be in charge of the candy concession. It is a small glass enclosed counter containing various chocolate bars arranged in rows. Patrons can look through the glass and point to what they want, and I reach in from the back and place the items on the counter. There are Crispy Crunch bars and Jersey Milk and Rolos, about fifteen varieties in all, priced at ten cents each. At one end of the counter is the Orange Crush machine and a stash of paper cups. And at the back is a large machine with whirling white popcorn continuously jumping around inside the glass enclosure. This gives the illusion that the popcorn is freshly made, but of course it isn't. The manager just empties a new cardboard box of the pre-made stuff into the opening at the top every once in a while. Somehow the motion and the smell make people think it is fresh. At the bottom of the popcorn machine is a little metal chute with a door that lifts up to allow the popcorn to fall out into a box. The boxes come flat in a stack and have to be put together by folding and tucking in the ends. It is a manoeuvre with which I soon become very adept.

Moments on a Staircase

We have a full house, and everyone wants to sample the goodies, so the line-ups are long. No one complains, though. They all seem thrilled to have this modern theatre in the midst of our little town. I see neighbours and friends and even my mother and father. I can tell by their smiles that they are proud of me, but I have no time for chit chat. The manager comes behind the counter with me and helps out at intermission when things get really busy, but somehow, I keep my cool. Later, when the show is over and we are closing up, I count the money and roll up the dimes and nickels and pennies in paper wrappers for the deposit bag.

The manager helps me and says we have done very well for that first night. He is the skinniest man I ever met, pale and sickly looking with no personality at all. His name is Clint. It doesn't suit him, especially compared to the only other Clint I know, a young Clint Eastwood who appears in several of our early films. Our Clint is a bit paranoid about the money in the snack bar drawer, so he comes around several times during the night to check that it is still there, removing some of the larger bills so I won't be tempted to do some pilfering, I suppose. Of course, this never occurs to me. I have never stolen anything in my life, even from my mother's purse, like some of my friends admit doing on occasion. Later, Clint figures this out and stops checking on me. He makes a big mistake, though, when in a moment of largess he says I can eat anything I want from the snack bar. I proceed to gain about fifteen pounds in the next few months. I try everything, but my favourite combination of goodies includes some popcorn and a mint patty followed by several red licorice twizzlers. I wash this down with a cup of the orange drink to which I soon become quite addicted. God only knows what it's made of.

The snack bar is located in the lobby at the back of the main auditorium. A low wall separates the lobby from the rows of seats which stretch on a steep incline down to the stage. Above the stage, a large screen covers the back wall. From my vantage point behind the snack bar, I can plainly see the entire screen. Perched on my little wooden stool I really have the best seat in the house, and between customers, I watch the movies, usually several times on successive nights. I laugh and cry and willingly suspend my disbelief as I see amazing things come to life before my impressionable young eyes. If the movie is particularly enthralling, I direct patrons to go back to their seats and return later for treats at intermission, lest they miss the most exciting part of the show.

"Go and sit down," I order. "You're missing the best part."

This is really for my own benefit, since I don't want to miss it myself. In some cases, after a few nights I can repeat the dialogue word for word with the actors, and if no one is looking I pretend that I am a star up there in that magical, celluloid world. My favourite role is Scarlett O'Hara in *Gone with the Wind*:

'*Oh Ashley, Ashley! You do love me. Oh Ashley, say you do!*'

I am not alone in the lobby. Clint stands by the ticket box where he receives the patron's tickets and tears them in half, placing one half in the large black box against which he leans his emaciated body. He always wears a dark suit and a white shirt with a conservative tie knotted around his scrawny neck. After the show starts he wanders around the theatre, up and down the two main aisles, checking for people sneaking in through the exit doors or kids making out in the back row. He puts a stop to these activities with a steely glare that belies his puny physique. He carries a long, menacing-looking flashlight which he whips out and brandishes at the offending folk, spotlighting their iniquities for all to see. On rare occasions, he orders them to leave and accompanies them to the door. Usually they are teen-agers who don't realize they could knock him over with a feather.

Clint does have a secret weapon, however. It's Johnny Armondo, the usher. Short and square and darkly menacing, Johnny often appears at Clint's elbow and makes sure the orders to evacuate are obeyed. He is the enforcer.

We all think he has some mysterious ties to the Mafia. No one knows for sure. We do know Johnny has body odour really bad. Maybe it is the smell of him that sends the guilty patrons scurrying for the door. Johnny and the other usher each have a uniform jacket. They are decorated like some kind of Prussian officer's uniform, with gold braid and large epaulets on the shoulders.

Bill Brown shares usher duties with Johnny Armondo on alternate nights. Bill is tall and gangly with long arms that hang out of his jacket. On Bill, the epaulets adorn his elbows rather than his shoulders, which are non-existent. Bill has a sea of red pimples all over his face and he and Johnny are very careful not to get into the wrong jacket; Johnny because he thinks Bill's acne might rub off on him and Bill because he can't bear the stench of Johnny's jacket, whose silk lining has started to rot away in the arm pit area. Both jackets hang in the men's washroom when not in use, and they eventually absorb some other odours of questionable origin.

Along with Clint and the usher "du jour", I share my space with a large, floor to ceiling mirror. Reflected in its depths is the glass cage in the outer lobby where the cashier sits. She is the *crème de la crème* of the Fox. Gail is a stunningly beautiful brunette who, more than a little, resembles Donna Reed in *From Here to Eternity*. She can be clearly seen from the street. Many a young man who has no intention of going to the show eagerly slides his quarter into the little round opening in the ticket booth so he can get a better look at her. It's a small price to pay for the hint of a smile on a gorgeous face and a sultry voice that says, "Welcome to the Fox. Enjoy the show."

I can see the cashier reflected in the mirror from my candy counter, but I can't hear her, so we communicate using sign language. When Mr. Di Salvo makes one of his unannounced appearances, the cashier is the first one to see him coming. She signals frantically to me in the snack bar, waving her arms and making a face like a deer caught it the headlights.

"Cheez it! The boss!" I whisper in my best Jimmy Cagney imitation. Then the usher buttons his jacket, Clint straightens his tie and I hide my mint patty and start to dust the top of the popcorn machine. Although he strikes fear into our hearts, for some reason, Mr. Di Salvo is always nice to me, remembering my name and asking how I like working here. Somehow, we seem to have bonded on the day he hired me, the day of the serendipitous dare, but I'm not sure why.

The final, and most irreplaceable member or out little theatrical group is Fred, the projectionist. He is a rumpled, middle-aged man who smells of alcohol. When I arrive for work, Fred is already upstairs in the projection booth and when I leave he is still there. Some of us speculate that he lives up there. He prepares the reels for the movie we are about to show. The film has little marks on the corner that are barely noticeable and this warns the projectionist when it is time to switch reels. Of course, this works only if he is paying attention. Often, Fred is not aware of this occurrence and the action on the screen comes to an abrupt halt accompanied by a flapping noise as the black ribbon of film goes round and round, waving crazily in the air. Inevitably the audience boos loudly, turning in their seats to glare up at Fred's hideaway, where a few choice expletives can be heard before the machine roars to life and the movie resumes.

Moments on a Staircase

After several of these slip-ups, Fred gets fired. He packs up and leaves in surly silence, but he always comes back and things go on as before. I don't know for sure, but I think he is related to Mr. Di Salvo by marriage; his mangia-cake brother-in-law, or something.

For showing up three nights a week and every other Saturday afternoon, I am paid the handsome sum of eight dollars. From this, my mom extracts three, one-dollar bills and tucks them into her apron pocket.

"Room and board," she says.

I never get a raise in pay but I manage to live on five dollars a week, and rather well. I would still be rich with the five dollars left in my pay packet if I didn't walk past Mather's jewellery store one day and see a beautiful gold Bulova watch in the window. It has a bracelet band made of little crescent moon-shaped pieces and I fall in love with it. Mr. Mather allows me to buy it *'on time'*, an unusual practice for the day, but I have to leave it in the store until it is completely paid for. Every week I give him five dollars, which, of course, leaves me with nothing. But I don't mind. When I make my weekly payment, Mr. Mather, if he isn't busy, takes the watch from the window and lets me look at it up close in its red velvet box. That is enough to keep me coming back faithfully for ten weeks until it's paid in full. I remember the day Mr. Mather takes it out of the window for the last time.

"There you go, dear," he says. It's all yours." He winds the little gold stem on the watch and adjusts the hands to the correct time. Then he fastens it to my eager wrist with great ceremony. Later I discover that this is not an easy task, but with a little practice I learn to do up the clasp with one hand and I wear it every day after that for a very long time.

Moments on a Staircase

I wear it to work at the Fox all through high school and even when I enter Teachers College in Hamilton. I never get a raise in pay but I manage to live on five-dollars a week rather well.

During these years several managers come and go. To everyone's amazement, Clint marries a local school-teacher and moves away. Then comes Audrey who is a wonderful boss and mothers us all, but she develops phlebitis from standing for so long and has to quit. Ushers and cashiers change too, until eventually, I am the grand old lady of the Fox. I have been there from day one and never missed a day of work. I even manage not to get fired when George Strong is hired as the new manager.

George is a tall, balding man in his early forties. He smokes foul-smelling cigars and hangs around the cashier's cage flirting with Gail. He doesn't bother much with me. He has a bad temper and loses it frequently, but I learn to ignore his tirades and tune him out. That is until the Johnny Armondo incident.

George calls all of the female employees together one day and makes an announcement.

"There's a new law pertaining to the children's matinees on Saturdays," he says. "Youse girls are to be called matrons, and youse'll hafta' wear uniforms. Mr. Di Salvo can't afford no uniforms, so youse'll hafta' wear the ushers' jackets on Saturday afternoons. There's two matrons for each show, and two ushers' jackets, so no problemo, eh girls?"

"I'm not wearing an usher's jacket," I say, thinking with horror of having to slide my body into the stink of Johnny Armondo's jacket.

I push the heavy door open and go outside. The other girls scurry after me, looking scared. George follows us out to the street, chomping down hard on the end of his cigar and glaring.

Moments on a Staircase

"You'll do what you're told, Missy," he growls.

"No, I won't. And you can't make me," I say, jutting out my chin and glaring back at him.

"Oh, yah? We'll see about that. If you won't wear that jacket on Saturday, then don't bother coming in. You're fired."

I feel the wind rush out of my chest and the lights of the marquis above my head start to dance before my eyes. Then, from somewhere deep inside, a great indignation spreads through my body. In a searing blast of courageous bravado, I draw myself up to stare into his eyes and I wave a finger under George's nose, nearly dislodging the smelly old stogie dangling from his lips.

"You didn't hire me, and you can't fire me!" I sneer. "Mr. Di Salvo hired me. I was here when you came, and I'll still be here when you're long gone." I turn on my heel and walk off down the street, leaving him to sputter in a cloud of his own smoke.

When I get home, I tell my mom and dad that I might have got myself fired. Mom is worried, but my dad is a staunch union man. He says I've done the right thing standing up for myself and my fellow workers.

When it's time for the matinee on Saturday, I lose my courage, but dad says I can't let the other girls down, so off I go, not knowing what to expect.

Much to my surprise, I'm met by a smiling George who proudly shows me the new white lab coats he has purchased for the matrons. It is my first real taste of power.

I feel really good until I try to put on one of the coats and can hardly get my arms into the sleeves, let alone do it up. Then I look at the size. Extra Small. That bastard! My arms are practically pinned to my sides, but I wear it anyway. At least it isn't Johnny Armondo's jacket. George laughs behind his cigar every time he looks at me squeezed into that coat.

But there is a God, and before too long George Strong is gone, and I am still plying my trade behind the candy counter. Then one night, it happens. I look up from rearranging the Babe Ruth bars to see the image of a good-looking guy in the lobby mirror. He is leaning in to talk to Gail in the cashier's booth, one foot casually braced on the door frame. I see his profile and I am stunned with the beauty of it. A noble nose, sculpted for some Roman emperor's bust, high and rounded at the bridge, sloping down to the delicately flared nostrils. His lips are full and sensuous, the upper lip curled slightly into an Elvis Presley sneer. I can't take my eyes off him. His hair is brown and wavy, arranged in a pompadour, and his side-burns are long, covering the high cheekbones beneath. His collar stands up around his ears, giving him a slightly dangerous look. The shoulders that fill out the jacket are large and his body tapers down to nicely fill out a tight pair of jeans. He wears cowboy boots under the flared legs of the pants. I am in love with this image in the mirror, and like the Lady of Shallot, I long to get a look at the real thing.

But I can see he is smiling at Gail and trying to charm her into something. She doesn't seem too interested. My heart leaps. After a while he leaves and I creep out of my snack bar to talk to her.

"Who is that good looking guy?" I ask.

"His name is Paul something-or-other," Gail says. "He's a fireman. He wants to take me out dancing, but I've danced with him before. He's a terrible dancer. Good kisser, though." She smiles, kind of sneaky-like.

"If you don't want him, can I have him?" I ask hopefully.

Moments on a Staircase

Gail looks at me in my navy skirt and white blouse, owly glasses on my nose, orange drink around the corners of my lips. She smiles condescendingly.

"Sure", she says. "You can have him if you like. But if he takes you dancing, honey, wear army boots."

On the night of Hurricane Hazel, Paul comes to the Fox with his friend Sam to pick Gail up. She is Sam's date. No one else is around, so Sam asks Gail to get me to go out with Paul. I practically run out of the Fox to get into the front seat of his gray, 1937 Chevy coupe. He doesn't talk to me as we drive off. We end up at the beach watching the waves crash up onto the shore of Lake Ontario in the worst storm to hit our area in decades. People are out filling sand bags in the dark, working by flashlight, trying to protect the shoreline. We sit and watch.

Gail and Sam start fooling around in the back seat. I hear their heavy breathing and a few moans. Finally, Paul seems to notice me. He slips an arm around my shoulders and kisses me. I have never been kissed before. My head is full of coloured lights exploding behind my eyes. I think I'm going to faint. Then he kisses me again, long and slow and I start to really enjoy all the sensations I'm feeling. By the time he takes me home, I am mad about him. My lips are big and puffy and sore. Who cares if he can dance?

As I walk through the front door, my dad pushes past me and heads for the driveway.

"Where have you been?" my mother says. "It's four o'clock in the morning. You got out of work ages ago. We've been frantic with worry."

"I had a date, mom. He's wonderful. I'm in love."

"Look at your lips. What have you been doing?"

Moments on a Staircase

I twirl dreamily around the ballroom a few times in my Scarlett O'Hara dress with the ruffled petticoat.

"We were filling sandbags at the lake. One of them hit me in the mouth. Where is dad?"

"He's gone to get that guy you were with and kill him."

Thank goodness, dad's old Plymouth can't keep up with the Chevy. Paul and I are married four years later. I get a job as a teacher and have to quit the Fox. It is a bitter-sweet moment. My salary increases ten-fold, but I miss the movies and the snacks and the people. Most of all, when people ask me what I do, I miss being able to say,

"I am *in the theatre!* "

Chapter 6 - My Brief Affair with Dimitri Metropolis

I met Dimitri Metropolis, conductor of the New York Philharmonic orchestra, in 1955 when I was sixteen and he was much older. But our story began many years before the affair itself. It all started in my mother's kitchen when my brother Don and I were told to do the dishes after supper. I was a rebellious ten-year old who wanted nothing to do with housework of any kind, so I usually protested loudly at this forced labour. My brother, on the other hand, was five years older; a kind, loving boy who understood our obligation to help out when we were asked. He was able to manipulate me into doing what I was told by turning the whole process into a game. This talent of his was put to good use in his later life as a United Church minister. I'm sure he got lots of practice for his calling by having a sister like me.

He would go to the sink and fill up the dishpan with hot, soapy water.

"Do you want to wash or dry?" he'd ask.

"Neither one," I'd say.

"Come on, Mare. We'll play the game."

"I'll wash," I would answer in a grumpy voice. Then I'd swish the dishcloth around making patterns in the bubbles while Don waited patiently for some dishes to dry. After a while I'd whine, "I don't want to wash any more." So, Don would trade places with me. He'd wash most of the dishes and place them in the rack to dry while I snapped the towel at his legs. After he had washed lots of dishes, I'd demand that we trade places again so he'd have to dry all the dishes he had just washed. It was a pretty good scam unless mother was watching.

I think Don just wanted to protect me from mother's wrath when he suggested we play a game. He was deeply engrossed in classical music at the time and spent many hours playing his albums or conducting an imaginary orchestra as he listened to *Saturday Afternoon at the Met* on the radio. I thought it was dreary caterwauling, but once in a while I'd hear something beautiful and Don would say, "Listen to this, Mare, listen to this." The game he contrived to keep me at the sink at least looking like I was helping, involved naming the conductors of some of the great symphony orchestras of the time and pretty soon I knew their names off by heart.

"Toronto Symphony", Don would say.

"Sir Ernest McMillan", I'd reply on cue, like a well-trained parrot.

"Boston Pops."

"Arthur Fiedler," I'd snap back.

"Good for you, Mare." Then, "New York Philharmonic".

"Dimitri Metropolis," my automatic rejoinder.

Moments on a Staircase

Every time he'd add a few new ones, just to keep me on my toes, until I knew the conductors of all the major orchestras of the world.

"London Symphony," he'd say, trying to stump me.

"Sir Thomas Beecham," I'd respond, without hesitation.

As we grew up we still played the game at random moments, just for fun.

"The Philadelphia Orchestra", Don would bark at me at the Christmas dinner table.

"Eugene Ormandy", I'd snap back. Then we'd laugh. It was our special thing. Unfortunately, we couldn't take it on the road, since no one else around us seemed to know what or whom we were talking about. It had very little value for party small talk. That is, until the Dimitri affair.

It was the custom at Saltfleet High School in Stoney Creek for grade twelve students to go on a supervised field trip to New York City. At sixteen, I signed up eagerly and checked in with some girl friends to the Robert Clay Hotel on Forty-Third street. It had been a swanky hotel at some time in its history, but was a bit run down and unspectacular when we arrived. Our room on the twelfth floor was adequate for four teen-age girls on their own for the first time in a big city. The window of our room looked out on the street and had no screen. I remember sitting on the windowsill peeling an orange and throwing the pieces out the window. We laughed as the people walking below ducked and looked up angrily at our window.

The hotel had elevator ladies who took us up and down, opening the door and then sliding the metal cage across with a white gloved hand to let folks in and out. We kids, of course, never tipped them, so they didn't like to accommodate us in any way. We were made to wait inordinately long periods for the elevator to get moving when we wanted to go up. And going down meant standing by the doors for ages while the cage creaked past our floor many times without even slowing down. Most of us got used to using the stairs on the way down. But twelve floors is a long way up. We learned to wait for some other passenger to get aboard and then slip on before the elevator Nazi could shut the door in our faces. That's what happened the day I met Dimitri.

I was lurking by the elevator in the lobby, half hidden by a potted palm, waiting for someone to come along when a short, rotund older man approached. As he entered the elevator, the operator snapped to attention and smiled at him. He acknowledged her greeting with a curt nod and took the newspaper from beneath his arm, opening it close to the thick glasses he wore. As he provided this diversion, I slipped from my hiding place and moved quickly to the back of the elevator. The operator glared at me as she closed the doors and moved her handle to the up position.

"Twelve, please," I mumbled politely.

Then, I observed my companion from behind. I could clearly see the top of his head where the hair was sparse, barely covering a pink scalp. His glasses were markedly thick and caused him to squint into the paper he was reading. A very ordinary little man, I thought.

In a few moments, I noticed we had skimmed past the twelfth floor and were heading higher.

"Twelve, please," I said in my loudest, most commanding voice.

Moments on a Staircase

The operator looked at me with a curled lip. "We are going to the penthouse for Mr. Metropolis," she announced emphatically. This familiar name triggered an automatic response from me.

"Dimitri?" I managed to choke out.

The little man looked up from his paper, turned and eyed me quizzically.

"The same," he pronounced solemnly, before going back to his reading.

When we reached the penthouse, the doors slid open and we were inside a vast space, beautifully decorated with statues of Greek gods in niches. A long hallway ended in a pair of gold trimmed French doors leading, I supposed, to the little man's inner sanctum.

He placed an unknown amount of money into the hands of the smiling operator, then exited the elevator, turning slightly to look at me with a bemused expression before the doors closed and he was gone.

All the way down to the twelfth floor I imagined how excited Don would be when I told him the news.

"I met Dimitri Metropolis in an elevator in New York City."

Moments on a Staircase

Chapter 7 - Paul Suits Blue

I should have stopped dead in my tracks as I walked down the aisle of Stoney Creek United Church on my wedding day, July 26, 1958. That's when I heard the sobs coming from Paul's side of the church where his mother and sister sat snuffling softly, arms around each other. But who could blame them? Their baby boy was being snatched away by this evil woman of the world who had hoodwinked him into marriage. To them, it was irrelevant that he was six years older than me, and ought to have known his own mind at twenty-five. They should have been cheering. I was nineteen, gainfully employed and even mildly attractive, and he was getting a bit long in the tooth for settling down. But to my new in-laws, who were *'holy rollers'*, I was a sinner who refused to be "washed in the blood", and "dyed in the wool", or whatever ecclesiastical cliché they claimed would rescue me from the path to ruin, which I was hurtling down at full speed.

No one would have blamed me for turning on my heel and leaving the church, if they had known about my stressful day up to that point, First, my dad cut his thumb to the bone at work and had bandaged it clumsily with about twelve yards of floppy gauze. Unfortunately, this was the hand I was to hold on the way down the aisle. Somehow we managed, with me gripping the end of the bandage which stood up like a beacon in front of us. I sincerely hoped the blood which had begun to seep out would not drip onto my white gown.

The second disaster was caused by a sailboat cruising at a leisurely pace beneath the lift bridge on the Burlington canal.

On the Toronto side of the bridge sat the Browns on their way to pick me up and take me to the church. My mom had asked her friend Hazel Brown to let me ride to the church in her lovely new car, since my dad's car was an old, blue 1947 Plymouth. The sailboat was in no hurry as it glided under the elevated bridge and the Browns were helpless to get to Stoney Creek any other way. The Skyway bridge was still in the design stages in 1958. So, they sat and stewed while we waited and worried at home.

Where were they? I knew if I was late getting to the church Paul might have second thoughts and fly the coop. Meanwhile, dad tried to clean up the back seat of his car just in case. He had transported two huge sacks of potatoes to the church hall that morning so mom's UCW friends could make potato salad for the wedding supper. Dirt from the sacks was all over the back seat of the car. Dad did the best he could, and at the last possible moment mom put a white sheet over the seat and I climbed in holding the skirt of my wedding dress up around my waist. The neighbours who had gathered to watch us depart looked on in amazement. Thank goodness my underwear was new and quite attractive--frilly pink trousseau panties instead of Watson's silk drawers, size-medium, which was what I usually wore.

We were quite late arriving. When we pulled up in front of the church, the usher in charge of parking tried to shoo us around to the back, thinking, I suppose, we were a group of indigent hillbilly relatives. Imagine his surprise when I tumbled unceremoniously from the back seat in a crumpled, slightly dirty-looking wedding gown.

Moments on a Staircase

I practically ran up the steps as Mr. Cline, the verger, pulled on the ropes to ring the big bells in the tower above. Paul said later that he was about to bolt but his best man, Rodger, held onto him and talked him down off the ledge.

This extra anxiety caused Paul to sweat profusely. When, at last, I arrived at the altar and took a sideways glance at him, I could see the beads of sweat standing out all over his forehead. His cheeks were red and his eyes were bloodshot. I thought he was hung over from his bachelor party the night before, so I was angry with him and refused to make eye contact. This feeling lasted most of the way through the ceremony. Rodger insisted in later years they had not been drinking the night before, and it was just the heat and nervous excitement that made Paul sweat.

When it came to the part where I had to say "I do," I looked up into Paul's big blue eyes and thought to myself, "Who is this guy?" I felt like I didn't know him from a hole in the ground. I certainly didn't remember his eyes being so intensely blue. Where did he get those eyes? Was it the dark blue blazer he was wearing that brought out the colour so vividly, or was it the beautiful blue tie he had borrowed for the occasion. Then it dawned on me that I had never really seen much of him in daylight. Most of our dates were at night up on lovers' lane or at the beach where his sunglasses masked his eyes. Was this really the guy I wanted to marry? And what did that mean? Who would do the cooking and the washing? Who would look after me when I was sick? Did he snore? How would we pay the rent?

God, let me out of here, I thought. The snuffling coming from the benches behind me stopped suddenly and was replaced by a kind of hopeful silence. It became very quiet in the sanctuary. Just the humming of the organ's inner workings could be heard, then some discreet coughing from my side of the church where my mother glared from under the brim of her new ostrich-feathered hat. I glanced at my dad who raised his bloody thumb slightly and smiled encouragingly at me.

Right then I realized I'd have to go through with it. We could get a divorce tomorrow, I reasoned. But for now, there was a lot of potato salad to eat and I knew potato salad would never keep in that heat.

"I do," I said.

And I did...for forty-three more years.

Chapter 8 - The Happiest Day of my Life

On January 16, 1963, when the doctor pulled my first baby out of my body with forceps and put him on my stomach, I remember such a feeling of unconditional love coursing through me as I gazed at my newborn baby boy.

As I drifted off to a well-earned sleep I could see he had cauliflower ears and a pointed head. But to me he was the most beautiful thing I had ever seen. I presume his deformities came from being wedged in the birth canal for three days where he had acquired a dusky hue from being diffused with blood when I stubbornly refused to let him go.

It all began seven months before, when Paul took me on a surprise trip.

"Pack your bags, honey," he announced one day. "We are going on a little holiday."

I envisioned Disney World or Myrtle Beach or some other exotic place.

"Where are we going?" I asked

Moments on a Staircase

"Around Lake Ontario," he said proudly. "We'll cross over at the Ivy Lea Bridge in Kingston and then go all the way around and back to Niagara Falls. What do you think of that?"

He looked so happy that I didn't have the heart to tell him where I thought we might be going. So we packed up and off we went. It was a long, long ride but we saw lots of trees and farms with cows in fields and even had the occasional glimpse of the lake shining in the distance. For lunch on the second day, we stopped in a little fishing village and I ate fresh clams at a small waterfront café. It was very quaint and charming, fishnet decorations and colourful buoys adorning the walls. When we stopped that night at a motel by the side of the highway, I was very ill. I was sure it was the clams. Paul put a quarter in a little slot on the electric bed thinking the rocking motion would soothe my stomach. It went on for hours and finally I slept on the floor. This was quite handy, because I could just crawl into the bathroom at toilet height when the spirit moved me. And it moved me several times.

By morning I was feeling a bit better, so Paul made reservations at a very fancy restaurant in Rochester, New York. We ordered expensive steaks and when they arrived at the table I took one look and ran outside to heave up my guts in the parking lot. Neither of us had any supper that night.

When we got home the next day, I was still feeling nauseous so I made an appointment with my doctor. I was sure my gall bladder was acting up again.

"Do I need to have it out?" I asked.

"Oh, it'll come out alright," the doctor laughed. "About seven months from now. You're pregnant."

Moments on a Staircase

Both Paul and I were thunderstruck. We had been married for four years and hadn't had any luck getting in the 'family way'. This was a miracle!

Looking back, I can honestly say it was a miracle I lived through it. I lay in the labour room for a long time listening to the cries of other women who came and went. It was interesting to hear what they said.

"That bastard had better not come near me again or I'll kill him with my bare hands!" one woman yelled. Thank goodness men were not permitted in the labour or delivery rooms. They would never have had sex with their wives again.

One lady obviously missed having her husband close by at this crucial moment in her life. I think she was Italian. "Gino, Gino, Gino," she intoned over and over again, each time her voice rising higher until it reached a crescendo in an eardrum splitting scream. There would be a few minutes of silence and then when the next pain came she'd start up again.

I tried to keep quiet but I'm afraid I, too, let go with a blood-curdling yell once in a while. The pain was in my back and I found out from a troop of nurses in training that this likely meant the baby was facing upside-down. These young Florence Nightingales liked to poke my swollen belly to feel the unusual position of the baby inside. Unfortunately, the prodding would bring on more pain. On my second day in this torture chamber, the group of nurselets were amazed to see me.

"Are you still here?"

"Stay away from me," I snarled.

"Where is her doctor?" one of them said.

"I think he has jaundice. They're looking after him in the doctor's lounge," someone answered.

"Who is looking after me?" I wailed, but no one was listening.

I heard the women in labour come and go all that night and the next day. When the sides of their beds clanged up and a crew of nurses pushed them out the door, I envisioned them going to the delivery room which I began to think of as 'the promised land.'

By the end of the second day, I had still not seen my doctor, or indeed anyone who was remotely interested in my fate. I could feel myself growing weaker and I started to hallucinate. Paul was coming to rescue me with the aerial ladder from the firetruck he drove at work. I could see him plain as day in the second story window of the labour room. By now, I was all alone there.

Finally, the head nurse came by and looked with consternation at my chart. Shortly after that, my doctor appeared at my bedside. He was yellow and had a nurse on either side of him to hold him up. With shaky hands he examined my stubborn bump and encouraged me to push. My foot was on his chest and when I gave a feeble push, he reeled backwards and had to be restored to my bedside by his attendants.

One of the nurses glared at me and said, "Come on now. A big strong girl like you should be able to push harder than that."

At that moment a cleaning lady came by with her bucket and mop. "She hasn't had anything to eat or drink for two days," she announced to the medical personnel gathered around my bed.

It was amazing how fast they clanged up the side of my bed. Thanks to this angel of mercy I was at last on my way to Heaven.

Moments on a Staircase

When I awoke, I was lying on a gurney in an elevator with a nurse standing nearby. In her arms was a small bundle wrapped in a blue blanket. And standing beside her, trying to peer under the flap of the blanket was Paul. His blue eyes were wide with wonder as he backed the nurse into a corner and, despite her protests, lifted the blanket to look for the first time at his son. I had never seen him look so proud and happy. Obviously, he was like me and didn't notice the strange appearance of our offspring. We were blinded by love.

My mother and father were allowed to visit the next day. They had been frantic waiting three days to find out what happened. Whenever they called the hospital an anonymous voice informed them that I was doing as well as could be expected.

"What the hell does that mean?" my father said. Mother had to restrain him from coming to find me. When they finally got to visit me, they were pleasantly surprised to see I was sitting up in bed with my lipstick on, smoking a cigarette.

I could hardly wait for my folks to come back from the nursery where the babies were kept for viewing through a large plate glass window. I was anxious to hear what they thought. I was sure they would say he was the most gorgeous baby ever born.

"Well, what do you think?" I asked. Mother hid her emotions well.

"He's beautiful dear," she said as she kissed my cheek. "So big and strong, just like his grandpa." She squeezed my hand and smiled reassuringly at me.

But my father had never mastered the art of diplomacy. He said nothing, but the look on his face made it plain how he felt. He came to the side of the bed and placed one of his huge, tire-building hands on the top of my head, patting me roughly. There were tears in his eyes, a sight I had never seen before, which I took to be tears of joy. He later admitted that he was horrified by the look of his grandchild--yellow, pointy headed, with forceps scars on his ears. He thought I had given birth to *Denny Dimwit*. But he managed to hold it together for me.

Whenever the baby was in my room for a feeding, everyone got evicted. His father didn't get to hold him until we finally took him home a week later. I sat beside Paul in the front seat of the car and held the baby so he could get a good look at him. No seatbelts, no car seat, just a baby in his mother's arms, daddy driving distractedly all over the road. I shudder to think of it now.

Of course, the good news is that somehow, we arrived safely at home and day by day our baby lost his jaundiced look. The pointy head was hidden by his little bonnet and then one day it was gone and some fine baby hair was growing there. Best of all, he had his father's big blue eyes. By the time he was two-months-old he really was the most beautiful baby ever born. I have the pictures to prove it. We called him Teddy.

Sometimes, when I look at my big, handsome, bearded son, who decided to call himself Ed when he was ten, I remember the happiest day of my life and wonder what ever happened to that beautiful little Teddy of mine.

Chapter 9 - The Happiest Day of My Life Part 2

Since we thought of our firstborn as a miracle, it never occurred to my husband and I that it could happen again. Lightning doesn't strike twice in the same place, they say. But it did for us. When Teddy was about fifteen-months old, my gall bladder began to act up once more. It was déjà vu all over again when we discovered we were expecting. Paul was happy and proud of his impending fatherhood, although he had the good sense to invest in a large economy-size box of condoms.

But I had a secret fear that I shared only with my mother.

"How can I love another baby as much as I love Teddy?" I asked.

She smiled a mysterious smile and said, "Don't worry about it. You will love this one too. It doesn't matter how many children you have. Your heart expands to allow you to love each of them just the same."

Even though she had three children of her own and appeared to love us equally, I knew in my heart she was wrong. I could never love any baby as much as I loved our Teddy. As I grew larger, I waited for my heart to expand as well, but it stayed just the same. I worried how I would hide this feeling so as not to hurt my new baby. I vowed he would never find out.

Moments on a Staircase

When the time came to go to the hospital I hid my pains from Paul. They were coming quite close together, but I was determined that I would not go to that place of torture until I absolutely had to. My best hiding place was inside the open fridge door. I pretended to be looking for something to eat so I could make faces and groan softly to myself without Paul noticing. It worked for a while, but at last I looked up after one enormous pain and saw a pair of anxious blue eyes staring at me over the top of the fridge door. The jig was up.

"Get your coat. We're going. . .NOW!" he ordered.

Paul loaded me into the car and drove like a madman to the hospital. The pains were coming thick and fast by the time we got there and I was taken immediately to the delivery room, where, about an hour later, my second baby boy was born. He popped out like the cork from a bottle of champagne. I was awake and aware of everything that was happening. I knew it was time to put on a happy face and pretend I was thrilled when they placed him on my stomach. And then another miracle occurred. I felt my heart swell with love for him, just as mother had told me it would. He was long and skinny, red in the face and screaming lustily, but once again I knew he was, without a doubt, the most beautiful baby I had ever seen. You can't fool with Mother Nature. She knows what she's doing.

We called this one Jaime. When we brought him home, we placed him in the bassinet my mother had made for Teddy. It was a basket standing on a sturdy wooden stool about three feet high. Mother had decorated it with the material from an old pair of dotted swiss curtains she had washed and starched. On each corner of the hood was a big satin bow.

By the time Jaime arrived, Teddy had been sleeping in a crib for quite a while, having rapidly outgrown this cute little bed. The first time we held Teddy up to look in the bassinet, he seemed fascinated by his new little brother. After a while, we tiptoed out of the nursery and closed the door behind us. Then we put Teddy down for a nap in his own room.

I guess Paul and I were tired from all the excitement of coming home and settling into a new routine with a baby and an active toddler. We fell asleep in the den watching television. Then something woke us and we sat up on instant alert. A strange noise was coming from the nursery. We both charged into the hall and were horrified to see the door was open. Paul got to the door first and put up his arm to stop me. We stared transfixed in horror at what we saw.

There was Teddy standing beside the bassinet which he had tipped over so that it rested on his sturdy little chest. He was holding it up with one hand. With the other, he poked a chubby finger at the baby's face. We were frozen to the spot, afraid to move in case we made him drop the bed, baby and all.

"Baby gots eyes," Teddy announced proudly. "Baby gots mouf."

We crept into the room and Paul moved quickly to rescue the baby from this precarious position propped up against his brother's chest.

We were not aware at the time, but this was the beginning of a brotherly bond that has lasted all their lives. Oh, they have had their moments, like all brothers do. But sibling rivalry is always secondary to the love they have for each other. Teddy always signs his birthday or Mother's Day cards, *From your favourite son's brother.*

Jaime, who now calls himself Jim, (*Jaime is a girl's name!*) admires his older brother and has always been proud of his accomplishments. The boys had a great relationship with their father. They spent a lot of time with him growing up and they were like the Three Musketeers. One for all, and all for one.

I was the odd man out in our little family. The only female in a masculine world. The boys vied for my attention sometimes and nothing I said would make them admit that I loved them equally. Their teasing was unmerciful.

I liked Erma Bombeck's solution when her children exhibited this rivalry for her affection. She wrote that she whispered in each of their ears, "I always loved you best." She said this made them happy and they stopped bothering her for the rest of her days. I decided to follow her lead, so I left a note in my cookbook that says, "Remember son, I always loved you best." I wonder what they'll say when they find it after I'm gone. I giggle every time I bake a cake.

Chapter 10 - The Halls of Academia

In 1967, when I was twenty-seven, I decided to continue my education, which had been interrupted by marriage, two kids and a full-time teaching job. I enrolled in a program of studies offered to mature students at McMaster University. Since most of us had jobs, classes were conducted after working hours at night and in the summer. My goal was to receive my BA. I'd like to say that I was interested in improving my mind, but it was actually because I found out that the new teacher in the classroom next to mine was earning five-thousand dollars a year more than me because she had a university degree. Greed inspired me. I started out attending classes on Tuesdays and Thursdays from six to ten in the evening, and adding on a few courses in the summer months. I majored in English Literature which involved much reading and writing many essays. Some of them I completed at the dining room table at four in the morning, while simultaneously attending to two kids throwing up with the flu. I had no time for supper on the nights I went to class, and I ploughed through snowdrifts in winter to get home to Binbrook before Paul had to go to work on the nightshift. I even fell into a huge ditch at McMaster that was being dug to connect the new nuclear facility to the science labs. Some kind stranger pulled me out of the ditch soaking wet, and I sat in class for two hours with steam rising from my pants, smelling like a wet dog. It took me ten, gruelling years to get to within three units of my goal.

I was determined to graduate in the fall convocation, so I looked for a 'bird course' to complete the requirements for my Bachelor of Arts. It didn't have to be English, since I had passed all the necessary courses for that subject. Something easy, I thought. And then I found it in the calendar--*The Possibility of Religious Belief* with professor D.B. Weeks. I had never taken a religious course before, but several classmates assured me the workload was not heavy and everyone passed. There were not even any books to purchase. All that was needed was a Bible, and if you didn't have one of your own, the Gideon Society would be happy to oblige. Or you could just steal one from any motel room.

On a hot July morning I found myself sitting in a classroom with about thirty other sweaty students. In the front row were three nuns, looking amazingly cool in their cumbersome attire; long flowing black robes, starched white wimples framing serene faces. We waited patiently for the prof to show up, not knowing what to expect. I pictured a saintly older man with a round smiling face, exuding kindness and love from every pore.

When he finally arrived, no one was prepared for Dr. Darren Bartholomew Weeks. Imagine if you can, the head of a fanatical John the Baptist, newly wrested from Salome's clutches, dark eyes darting around the room, taking stock of this class full of infidels. His cheeks were sunken hollows in a gaunt, spectral face. And to complement his looks, the head was attached to Ichabod Crane's body encased in a tattered black robe that flapped about as he moved his arms like a scarecrow in a corn field. The sight of this apparition was greeted by a terrified silence.

"Do you believe in God?" he thundered to the room at large as he slammed his briefcase down on the desk. We were too startled to respond and sat mesmerized by this man who would be spending the next six weeks with us. I'm sure I was not the only one who surreptitiously checked the calendar to see if it was too late to find another course, but unfortunately nothing else was available.

I can do this, I reassured myself. It's this or I don't graduate in October with that hefty raise in pay.

Dr. Weeks proceeded with his lecture, wafting about the room, up and down the aisles, talking all the time and occasionally punctuating his remarks with a question for one of his students. No one dared to look at him lest they be chosen to face the music.

"What about the question of evil in the world?" the wild doctor roared. "How do you explain evil if there is an all-powerful, almighty God? He pointed to a hapless fellow in the last row who had been trying anxiously to hide by sneezing into his handkerchief.

"I don't know," the poor guy managed to croak before another bout of sneezing rendered him incoherent.

"Don't know? You don't know?" thundered the good doctor, leaning down to glare at the object of his derision.

"Heretic," he bellowed. "What are you doing in my class if you don't know such a simple tenet of the Christian faith?" He whirled around and pointed to one of the nuns. His manner softened a little as she fumbled nervously with her rosary beads. "Take your time, my dear," he said.

"The Lord works in mysterious ways His wonders to perform," she managed to whisper as she crossed herself several times.

Moments on a Staircase

"Thank you, Sister," said the professor, smiling for the first time. Then his expression changed to a malevolent glare as he found me cringing at my desk, trying to make myself small and invisible. "And what about you, Miss? What do you think about this universal problem of evil?"

I straightened myself up and stared back at him. I heard words coming out of my mouth. I had no idea from whence they came.

"I suppose if I believed in all this I would say it was because of the notion of free will which God gave to man. That's why there is evil in the world. He can't really step in and fix it or else we wouldn't have free will."

A sneer of magnificent proportions twisted the doctor's features into a mask of contempt. "So," he purred, bringing his nose to within a drop of sweat of mine, "I see we have an unbeliever in the group. Well, well. I'm sure we'll all be ever so grateful if *Madam Agnostic* here would deign to share her incredible knowledge of the infinite with us." His voice oozed with sarcasm.

I stood my ground, staring back at him, but inside I was in agony. I could see my B.A. floating away on the summer breeze. Why had I said what I did? Why didn't I think of some religious cliché like the nun before me. I was sure that the *Possibility of Religious Belief* was quickly turning into the *Impossibility of Graduating* at the fall convocation. I don't remember much else about that first encounter, but I know from that time on I was known to all and sundry as, 'Madam Agnostic'.

Dr. Weeks retreated in triumph from out little confrontation. "Who here believes in the literal translation of the Bible? Was the world really created in seven days, or is the Bible incorrect? His burning gaze swept the cowering members of the class.

"God inspired the word, so it must be correct," piped up Sister Antoinette who was fast becoming teacher's pet.

"So they say," answered Dr. Weeks with a smile of approval. Then turning on his toes to accost me as I tried to hide in my corner desk, he said "But let us consult *Madam Agnostic*. What do you have to say about this matter? Is the Bible divinely inspired or a load of hogwash?"

I didn't care any more. I knew my B.A. had slipped out of my grasp and was floating away, gone with the wind. Besides, he made me mad.

"I think with all the different translations and undue influences on the translators, there is some room for error. Maybe it's like free will. Maybe God couldn't maintain control over all that was written in the Bible."

"And you know this how?" he said, turning to include the rest of the class, who followed his lead and stared disapprovingly at me.

"I don't know. I just wonder, is all. It seems there might be a possibility of human error here," I said.

"Might there, *Madam Agnostic*? Or might you be missing the faith necessary for religious belief? Might you just be a skeptic who believes in nothing but what she can see with her own eyes, hear with her own ears?"

"I guess I'm a *Doubting Thomas*," I said, sticking out my chin defiantly.

And so it went throughout the six-week course. Everyone in the class called me *Madam Agnostic* and the nuns scurried past me in the hall and wouldn't sit near me at break time in the cafeteria. Not a class went by that I was not forced to give my opinion on the topic under discussion. I must confess, I sometimes enjoyed our little encounters, but it was clear I was no match for Dr. Weeks. He could out quote me, out shout me and out think me any day of the week. Sometimes I had to fight back tears of humiliation that threatened to spill over and run down my cheeks. I stayed in class only because I was stubborn and because I clung to the rumour that no one ever failed a religious course. I desperately hoped it was true.

There was no final exam. An essay and class participation were the two main criteria for passing, and after all those English courses, I damn well knew how to write an essay. But class participation? Would it be enough, given that he had picked on me the entire time, calling me *Madam Agnostic* and holding my arguments up for ridicule. I waited anxiously for the final results to be posted on the door outside our classroom on the last day.

When I arrived, a large group was gathered near the door and I couldn't see the list. Someone ahead of me commented that the names on the list were those who passed and they were in order of merit, from highest to lowest. I needed a fifty to pass. When I got close enough to see the last few names on the list my heart sank. Mine was not there. Then I looked higher, it was not there either. I must have failed.

Suddenly, I heard someone laughing out loud.

"Look at the first name on the list. It's *Madam Agnostic*. She got a ninety-eight."

Everyone broke into applause as the group opened ranks to let me through. I saw for myself that my name was at the top of the list. I was incredulous. How could this be?

I thought Weeks hated me and I had been sure I wouldn't pass. Maybe there is a God, after all, I thought.

Moments on a Staircase

On graduation day, November 11, 1977, I was herded into a large gymnasium with about three hundred others. We were dressed in long black robes and given instructions about what to do. Since there was a shortage of Bachelor of Arts hoods to wear over the robes, we had to share. We entered convocation hall through the main doors at the back and someone threw a hood over us. Then we proceeded down the aisle to the front where the President of the University and some other dignitaries stood on a raised platform. One by one we were called to go up the stairs to receive our diplomas. When I got there, it was Dr. Weeks himself in his threadbare robe who stepped forward and shook my hand. He leaned down and smiled directly into my eyes.

"Congratulations, *Madam Agnostic*." he said, placing a scroll of vellum tied with a red ribbon into my hand. I clutched it eagerly in my sweaty palm.

I wanted to say something profound but someone took my arm and propelled me toward the down stairs. "Thank you," I called over my shoulder. As I headed back up the aisle toward the door I glanced up at the balcony where my mother and father sat with Paul. They were beaming proudly at me. I tried to wave, but my hand got caught in the huge sleeve of my gown so I just smiled back at them. I couldn't stop smiling.

When I got to the doorway, someone jerked the hood off my shoulders and threw it over the head of another graduate heading the other way. Then an unseen hand shoved me along in the lineup heading back to the gym.

A photographer was taking individual pictures in one corner, so I got in the queue to have my picture taken. As I got closer, I noticed the woman having her picture taken was holding a huge bouquet of red roses. I worried that I didn't have any flowers, but my fears were groundless. The photographer snatched them away from her, and when I sat down he threw them into my lap. He ordered me not to smile, but I couldn't help it. I had done it. I had graduated with a Bachelor of Arts from the Universitensis McMasterensis, *with all the rights and privileges thereof*. It said so right on my certificate. I was ecstatic.

After I had divested myself of the borrowed robe and got ready to go find my family, I realized that all this excitement had made me want to pee really badly. I found a washroom and sat down. On the wall of the cubicle was a rusty toilet tissue holder that dispensed single sandpaper sheets. Above it some anonymous smartass had scrawled, *B.A.'s, Take one!*

But at the end of the month when my next paycheck arrived, I had the last laugh.

Chapter 11 - The Equestrienne -

1980

Hitler would have been proud of Ingrid Kohn. Pure Aryan from the crown of her blonde, bullet-shaped head to the toes of her polished leather boots. Standing. in the centre of a ring of amateur riders mounted on their hired hacks, cracking her cat-o-nine tails against her jack-boot in time to the orders she issued from her humour-less lips.

"Squeeze mitt the thighs and the horse vill valk forvard into the bit," she ordered.

"Now close the hands firmly on the reins, and you are in control."

Squeezing and closing as we had been told, we guided our horses into the semblance of a circle around the edge of the arena.

Crack!

"Now ve vill trot. Up, down, up, down, up, down," Ingrid shouted.

Moments on a Staircase

The whip resounded: Crack! Crack! Crack!

Saddles creaked and horses exhaled in steamy compliance with Ingrid's commands, their ears nervously twitching in time with her voice and the sound of the crop slapping leather. My horse added a noisy "oomph" to the proceedings every time my rear end collided with the saddle.

Up, down (oomph), up, down (oomph)!

Since I was forty and already feeling large and awkward compared to the twelve-year-olds who were my fellow students, this added *oomph* was, to say the least, embarrassing. What had possessed me to ask for riding lessons for my fortieth birthday? I eased up on the down beat, using my legs to keep me up off the saddle.

Up, almost down, (oomph), up, almost down, (oomph)!

After a few circuits of the arena, my legs began to shake and I could feel the muscles of my thighs getting ready to let go. And to make matters worse, the horse was still oomphing loudly with each manoeuvre.

"Mary!" Crack. "Up, down, up, down."

The voice from the centre of the ring was shrill. I had not fooled Ingrid with my secret move. Somehow, she knew I was cheating on the down stroke. It reminded me of when I tried to get my dog, Max, to sit, and she would go through the motions with her bum wavering tentatively just inches above the floor, not touching it at all, big innocent brown eyes staring up at me. I tried to imitate Max as I turned to Ingrid with a puzzled expression intended to say, *who, me?*

And then I heard the words no student of Ingrid's ever wanted to hear.

"Mary!" Crack, crack! "You vill come into the centre of the ring please."

Oh, God. Two cracks. I knew I was in big trouble.

In my anxiety, I pulled on the wrong rein, heading my horse against the arena wall instead of into the middle where I had been ordered to appear. Fortunately, the horse knew better and turned himself around.

He walked toward Ingrid, ears up, head high, looking alert and slightly apologetic. After all, it wasn't his fault he had an idiot on his back.

"Vut ver you doing, Mary?" Ingrid said, glaring up at me suspiciously.

"Nothing," I said, trying to emulate Max's innocent demeanour, but without the aid of her big brown eyes. It didn't work. Ingrid's lip curled into a sneer.

"Ve haf vays of finding out what you are doing up on that horse, Mary", she said. "You are not fooling me ant you are not fooling zis horse. You are not landing on the saddle when you come down. Zis I know!"

She stared at me, eyes narrowed into slits of icy blue. "Ven I say up down, I mean up down, not up, half-way down. Do I make myself clear?"

"I'll try." I said, but I didn't have much hope.

Back I went to the circle, up, down, up, down, around and around. My companions seemed to be having no trouble at all. Their lithe young bodies began to fit with the horse, melding with its powerful movements as we jogged around the arena. I saw them relaxed and even smiling at each other. Ingrid was smiling too as she watched her supple students moving as one with their mounts.

I wanted to do that too. But I was so used to holding myself up off the saddle, I didn't ever feel like a part of the horse. I was simply a cork, bobbing up and down awkwardly on the waves, at total odds with the horse's movements. And my legs were burning with the effort of keeping myself afloat on top of that big, equine tsunami. I caught Ingrid peering at me when we rounded the end of the arena and entered her visual field, but thankfully she didn't single me out again.

After what seemed an eternity of pain and discomfort, Ingrid ordered us to stop, and I gratefully lowered my aching body onto the saddle, as my horse uttered one last enormous "oomph!".

"Now, because you haf done so vell mitt ze trotting, ve vill do sumting fun. It is called, *Around ze Vorld.*"

My classmates clapped their hands with excitement while I waited with growing apprehension.

"First ve shake our boots out of ze stirrups, ant zen ve turn around on ze saddle so ve are backvards."

"Oh, great!" yelled the youngsters.

"Zen, ve keep on going until ve haf turned all ze vay arount and ve are back facing frontwards again. See? Around ze Vorld." Ingrid cracked her whip to emphasize the unimaginable fun of it all.

My companions enthusiastically kicked off their stirrups and began to whirl around on their saddles, giggling and spinning with delight. Even the horses seemed to be getting a kick out of the game, tossing their heads and giving off horse laughs at each other.

Moments on a Staircase

My horse turned his head until one eye met mine with a dubious look. Not wanting to be singled out again I managed to get enough feeling into my lower legs so that I could drag my feet out of the stirrups. Lifting my right leg up over the horse's neck proved to be almost impossible, but with a last minute Herculean effort, I managed it. Now, I was sitting side-saddle with both feet hanging down. Try as I might, I could not lift the other leg up over the horse's rump. It just hung there, limp and helpless.

And then to my horror I felt myself sliding down on my back off the slippery leather saddle, slowly, slowly, my legs pointing straight down at the ground beneath my horse's feet. I tried to hold on with the cheeks of my bum, my elbows, my shoulder blades, my hair, but slowly, inexorably, I sank closer and closer to the ground. And then gravity took over and I was plummeting to earth like a stone. Down, down, down. Way down. Who knew horses were so tall?

But that wasn't the worst of it. When at last my feet hit the ground, I kept going. My numb and useless legs crumpled beneath me and I dissolved into the sawdust, perilously close to a pile of horse manure, in a heap of pain and humiliation.

I was so grateful to be back on the ground, however, that I didn't care when I saw Ingrid's boots striding toward me, heard the crack of her riding crop against her leather-encased calf. I knew the game was up.

"Vell, vell, Mary," Ingrid said, rocking back and forth on her heels. "I see you haf learned to dismount. Good for you. One step at a time zey say.

"*First Poland, then the rest of the vorld!*"

Did I really hear her say that? I don't know for sure. Maybe I was in shock from my long descent from the world's tallest horse.

But one thing I do know, I saw just a hint of a smile in those blue eyes of hers.

After such a disastrous first lesson in horsemanship from Frau Khon at Jack Mellow's Riding Academy in Ancaster, one might assume I would give it up and find some other way to amuse myself in middle age. Like playing a rousing game of bridge with friends, or bowling with the ladies church league from Binbrook. But you would be very wrong! You see, this desire to be a horsewoman was not a fleeting, pre-menopausal whim, not some hot flash impulse newly acquired along with a few grey hairs and several hormonal irregularities. Oh no. I had wanted to ride for a very long time. In fact, my horse history goes way back to the time when I was a little girl in 1946.

In those days my grandfather operated a small farm in Stoney Creek. Five acres of market garden, complete with a greenhouse, an outhouse and a barn which, as it happens, also served as a horse house. Grandpa always had a horse to do the ploughing, and her name was always Queenie. She might be brown or white or grey, but she was usually some old plow horse on her last legs, making a stop at grandpa's place before her inevitable final destination at the glue factory. I'm not sure why she was always called Queenie. Maybe grandpa had been in love with someone named Queenie when he was young. Or maybe it was his pet name for grandma, although I doubt it. No one in the family had heard them say two kind words to each other in forty years.

More than likely it was just that grandpa's memory wasn't too sharp, and since none of the Queenie's lasted very long, it was easier for him to remember one name for all of them, like he did for his granddaughters, whom he referred to as "Honey Bunny Boo." All six of us.

Moments on a Staircase

When I visited the little farm as a girl of six, my first stop was always Queenie's stall in the barn. It wasn't a box stall, just a standing stall big enough for one, and that's where she spent her time all winter, munching hay from her manger and looking out the little window through the dirt and cobwebs, trying to catch a glimpse of the outside world. I like to think she was happy when I put my small hand on her huge rump and said, "Git over, girl." I would give her a friendly slap the way I'd seen grandpa do, and she would let out a tired snort and heave her massive body one step over so I could walk up beside her and look her in the eye. It was heady stuff, this feeling of power over such an enormous beast.

I think it must have been a pleasant diversion for her, as I curry-combed her tangled mane and brushed the straw dust off her broad, sway back. Once in a while, she would show her appreciation by turning to slobber on my arm with her big, whiskery lips. When the snow began to melt, I often went outside, found a patch of long grass and brought it back to her for a treat. From the way she devoured it, I think she liked it very much. Having that little taste of green must have given her hope that spring at last was on its way.

While I worked, brushing and combing, I talked to her and told her my troubles. Once, when my other grandpa died, I put my face against Queenie's warm neck and let the tears flow, tears I had been hiding from my family for days. She seemed to understand, and gave me a sympathetic nudge with her soft, velvety nose.

I remember a day in early spring when, for the first time, grandpa asked me if I'd like to take her for a ride all by myself. He usually walked around with me, but this time I was to take her out alone. After all, I was six now. When he boosted me up on her back and put the halter rope in my hands, I was dizzy with excitement, being so high off the ground.

"Just give her a 'gee' or 'haw' and when you want to stop say 'whoa'," grandpa said

Then he led her outside, gave her a slap on the rear and off we went through the orchard at top speed. Please recall, Queenie had been standing still in her stall for five months. Imagine also, the legs of a six-year old child are not long enough to grip a horse of any size, let alone one with Percheron proportions like Queenie.

I hung on for dear life as we thundered through the small orchard where the trees were just coming into bud, branches whipping my face as I bounced along, legs sticking straight out, hanging onto a handful of mane and the halter rope with all my might.

"Whoa! Whoa!" I yelled, but Queenie was lost in the freedom of the moment, stretching her old legs into the wild gallop she had been dreaming of all winter. And who could blame her when we got a bit too close to a cherry tree and I was plucked off her back and deposited on the ground, still clinging to the rope. I'm almost sure she didn't do it on purpose, because she did eventually come to a stop before she had dragged me more than a furlong or two in the dirt. Looking behind her, she seemed a bit surprised to see me there.

I wasn't hurt, but my pride had been severely damaged, and I was angry with Queenie. How could she do that to me when I was so good to her?

"Goddammit," I said, just the way grandpa would have done. I got to my feet, dusted off the seat of my overalls and looked up at her back which was now well beyond my reach. Determined to regain my seat, I tried a few times to pull myself up by grabbing a handful of mane, but my arms were not strong enough. What would I do?

I spied a tree with a nice wide crotch and led Queenie over close beside it. She watched with amusement as I climbed up the tree and launched myself at her back. At the last moment she took a small sidestep away from the tree and I ended up on the ground. After three or four tries and several 'goddammits', I gave up. What was I to do now? Walk her back to the barn in disgrace? Grandpa would tell everyone and they would never let me forget it. Then I noticed the drainage ditch running through the orchard.

I tried to push a reluctant Queenie down into the ditch, but she refused to budge. I guess it looked pretty deep to her. So I went down into the ditch myself to show her it was okay. I then yanked on the halter rope and pulled her down with me. An enormous hoof landed right on top of my left foot. I felt my shoe sinking into the soft mud at the bottom of the ditch.

"Get off," I yelled, trying to pull myself free. "Gee, haw, ow!" Queenie just looked at me with a dumb expression on her face. Meanwhile, I felt fifteen hundred pounds of horse pressing on my poor foot. Finally, I remembered something I'd heard grandpa say to her.

"Back, girl, back!" I shouted, pushing on her chest with my fists. Slowly she backed up, releasing my foot.

I scrambled up and stood beside her on the edge. Now she was low enough for me to climb onto. Being withers deep in the ditch kept her from doing her little sidestep trick. With a good grip on her mane, I vaulted up on her back and proceeded to coax her to climb up out of the ditch. My foot was numb, my butt was sore, but other than that, no harm done.

On the way back home, Queenie was the model of good manners, walking politely along between the rows of trees, not even slowing down as she grabbed a cherry bud or two off the branches we passed. I guess she had satisfied her spring urge to be frisky as a filly for a few moments in her dull life.

"Hi, Honey Bunny Boo," grandpa said, when he saw us come into the barn. "How was your ride?"

"Okay," I said.

I didn't really trust him after that.

From that day on I was renowned in my family as an accomplished horsewoman. At the annual family picnic, grandpa would put his arm around me and tell the story to anyone who would listen:

"Goddammit, this here girl is a born rider. She took old Queenie for a gallop in the orchard one spring day with no saddle, no bridle, just bareback with a halter rope. And she brought her back safe and sound. And she was only six-years-old at the time, my Honey Bunny Boo. What do you think of that?"

My mother would turn pale and glare at grandpa, but the rest of the family would nod and say, "Mary knows her way around a horse, that's for sure."

Luckily, for many years I managed to avoid any situation that involved climbing on top of one of those frightening creatures.

After all, I had felt the strength and weight of that beast right down to my toes. For the remainder of my youth I avoided pony rides at the fair and even chose to sit in the little carriage on the merry-go-round instead of on one of the horses that went *up and down*. Still my reputation as an equestrienne had acquired a life of its own and lived on in the family lore.

Somehow, I managed to carry off this subterfuge until the summer I was thirty-five, when I went on a trip to Banff, Alberta with my husband Paul, and our two sons, Ed and Jim. As a surprise to me, Paul booked a trail ride, up to the top of a mountain near Lake Louise. What could I do? I had to go, or they'd know I'd been a phony all this time.

It was my moment of truth. I could almost hear Queenie laughing!

1975

I stood in the parking lot of the Chateau Lake Louise gazing in horror at the snow-capped mountain rising like a rocky pile of doom on the other side of the lake. The guide, a lanky young man named Walt, who was to lead our small band of tourists on a trail ride, was explaining that we were going to follow a path around the lake and then ascend to a tea house located on a little outcropping of rock just below the icy peak. He pointed almost straight up. I was terrified. Even the boys, who were ten and twelve, looked a bit alarmed at the size of the sheer cliff. It seemed to rise up out of the lake thrusting itself skyward until its top vanished in the clouds. But their father quickly allayed their fears.

"Don't worry boys," said Paul. "Your mother will be with us, so it'll be all right. Just watch her and do what she does. Remember, she's been riding since she was six." The boys relaxed then, apparently confident that their mother, the equestrienne, would protect them from all harm.

"Oh no," I thought. "After all these years I'm going to be found out. My kids and my husband will know I'm a fraud." I knew I had to figure out a way to save face. It was either that, or never hear the end of it from my family.

Moments on a Staircase

There were twelve of us gathered outside the hotel, twelve brave souls who had put themselves into the hands of Walt and his fellow wrangler, a taciturn fellow by the name of Kit. We were lined up side by side in front of Walt as he looked us up and down, his weather-beaten face inscrutable under the brim of his well-worn felt cowboy hat. I squirmed in my ragged jeans and an old plaid shirt of Paul's under my sweater as Walt stared at me. The boys and Paul were wearing only running shoes, jeans and lightweight tee shirts, as were most of our companions. One woman stood out in this ill-dressed gaggle of would-be cowboys. She was actually dressed in riding gear; jodhpurs and a black velvet jacket over a crisp white shirt, proper calf-length boots with large square heels, and a pair of leather gloves. We were all impressed with the professional look of her as she stood confidently beside us. Her name was Alison, and to complete her obvious superiority over the rest of us dowdy dudes, she spoke with a crisp and cultured British accent.

"I ride English," she said

"Not here you don't," drawled Walt.

As he walked back and forth, eyeballing his charges, Kit led the horses out, one at a time and Walt would allocate each animal to one of us. No one knew the secret formula Walt was using to match us up. Just as I had become convinced size was the criteria, he assigned a small, low-slung horse to the tallest man in the group. Then I thought perhaps it was temperament. But the beast who came prancing out, practically dragging Kit along with him, was handed over to a timid, little, middle-aged woman who looked terrified of her prize. We were all interested to see what kind of creature would be selected for Alison. Walt tried several times to match her up, but after walking around and lifting up the animal's hooves, or looking into its mouth, she rejected each one with an imperious shake of her head.

Moments on a Staircase

"Not this one," she scoffed.

At last, a rangy chestnut hunter met with her approval and she swung herself up into the saddle without any help from Kit. I gazed in admiration at her dexterity, and at the magnificent look of her up on that horse. She seemed almost ready to yell *tally-ho* as she galloped off, after a fox. Paul had been matched with a handsome black carriage horse who moved with precision and dignity around the compound. The boys each had a scrappy little mustang and they climbed aboard and waited eagerly for the ride to begin.

There were only two of us left with no mounts when Kit came out leading a gentle, sweet-faced, gray mare. She seemed calm and quiet, just my kind of horse. She even turned and looked at me directly with her kindly brown eyes and I could tell we were a match made in heaven. I was stunned when the woman beside me was summoned to her side and helped up into the saddle.

Now I was alone, all eyes watching and waiting impatiently for me to be hitched up with a horse. Kit conferred with Walt and they both stood for a moment eyeing me, heads tilted to one side, speaking softly to each other. I held my stomach in and tried to look leaner and fitter than I was. Then Walt nodded and Kit headed into the barn.

He came out leading a sway-backed, gray-whiskered old hack, who stumbled a few times on the anthills in the paddock. I watched in horror as he stood beside Walt, head down, dozing in the early morning sunshine. Walt grinned at me and beckoned.

"Mary, this here is Clem. He'll be your horse today."

Oh shit, I thought. Clem looked like he wouldn't make it out of the corral, let alone up the side of that mountain. Not wanting to make a scene, I obeyed orders and walked up beside Clem, giving him a pat on the nose. He cracked open one rheumy old eye and looked at me with resignation. I could imagine him thinking, *Oh no, another fat one. I'm too old for this.* It took both cowboys to get me up on Clem. He sidestepped each time I tried to throw my leg over the saddle, leaving me with one foot on top of him and the other twisted in the stirrup. I remembered Queenie having perfected this move, but I couldn't see a ditch anywhere in view, so Kit leaned against one side of Clem while Walt heaved me up into the saddle. My cheeks were red with the shame of it. Alison tried to hide her smile behind her gloved hand.

By now the others were impatient to be off. Alison was trotting around the enclosure, posting perfectly, just the way I had always imagined myself doing. As Clem stood dreaming, Walt mounted his own horse and pulled up alongside me.

"Old Clem's a real experienced climber," he said. "You don't have a thing to worry about. Just one little quirk he has. He don't like to be last on the trail, so keep up with the others, in the middle of the pack, eh? Have fun."

Fun? You've got to be kidding, I thought, as Old Clem shambled along the trail. Soon he maneuvered his way into the middle of the long line of horses and settled down to a slovenly stroll, banging his hooves against stones and outcroppings along the path. He didn't seem to have the strength to pick up his feet, dragging them along with each step. After a while, when I realized he likely wasn't going to trip and fall, I began to relax a bit. My boys were three or four horses ahead and every once in a while they would turn and wave happily at me. I even got so I could loosen my death grip on the pommel of the saddle and wave back. The terrain was fairly flat as our little caravan wound around to the other side of Lake Louise where our ascent would begin. The mountain we had to climb was reflected in the still, turquoise waters, an ominous reminder of what was yet to come.

Moments on a Staircase

As we meandered along Clem dozed, resting his nose on the rump of the horse in front of us, waking up occasionally to grab a mouthful of grass. I saw Walt up ahead riding point, and behind me Kit bringing up the rear as he chatted with Paul, who seemed to have his horse well in hand. A wave of optimism washed over me. Maybe I would get away with my reputation intact after all. All I had to do was hang on and pray. How hard could that be?

As Clem and I moseyed along the trail, I became so relaxed that I could actually take my eyes off the ground now and then to look around at the magnificent scenery. Spilling down from between two mountains on the opposite side of Lake Louise was the Victoria glacier; its enormous, snowy shoulders covered in a coat of diamonds sparkling in the sun. This was the same iconic view I had seen many times on calendars or postcards, but in reality, it was even more impressive. I began to feel glad I had come along.

After about twenty minutes, I saw Walt and the riders at the front of the line disappear around a bend in the trail and appear again slightly above me going in the opposite direction. When I got to this spot, I could see the trail made a hairpin turn and doubled back, climbing upward as it went. The kids looked down on me and waved happily. As we made the turn, Clem looked up and stopped for a moment, remembering, I suppose, what lay in store for him. But when the horse in front of us got a few yards ahead of him, Clem gave a snort of alarm and shuffled along a bit faster to catch up.

The trail became narrower at this point, and the horses strung themselves out in single file. Their hooves kicked up loose stones and sent them cascading down the trail under the feet of the horses that followed. Clem continued to stumble along as his feet rolled over the stones, sending me rocking back and forth in the saddle. I resumed my grip on the pommel and gritted my teeth.

Moments on a Staircase

Half an hour later, the trail had narrowed even more and seemed barely wide enough for a horse. We had passed many switchbacks, each one turning more abruptly than the last, and with each turn we climbed higher and higher. By now, the low bushes and large rocks that had protected us at the edge of the trail had disappeared. Looking down the granite cliff, there were no physical barriers between the top of the horse and the bottom of the mountain, miles below. Not so much as a blade of grass stood between us and disaster. It seemed to me Clem was deliberately leaning out over this abyss as we scrambled along, probably hoping I would fall off. By now he was puffing audibly and having trouble staying upright as he stumbled over the loose rocks that kept rolling by. I wondered how many of his former riders had ended up in a broken heap at the bottom of the precipice.

Try as I might to be brave, panic began to set my stomach in motion. But I was determined not to show it. I managed to muster enough maternal instinct to look up to see how the boys were making out. They were hanging on tightly now and their sturdy, sure-footed little horses seemed to be making steady progress up the mountainside. At least, I thought, when Clem and I hurtle to our doom, we won't wipe out the boys on the way down. Unfortunately, Paul, riding behind us, was right in our line of fire.

Riding close behind Walt at the head of our troupe was Alison. Her leggy steeplechaser seemed to be having no trouble with the ascent, but I noticed something unusual. Walt was now holding the reins of Alison's horse in one of his hands. She had a death grip on the pommel of her saddle and was looking rather green around the gills. The sight of her petrified face cheered me up for a moment, but only until the next switchback when the trail became impossibly steep. Old Clem dug in his hooves and heaved himself up step by step while I closed my eyes and prayed.

After another half hour of this torture, the top of the mountain was at last in sight. We had arrived at a small plateau where many years ago some entrepreneurial mountain goat had built a picturesque little gingerbread tea house. Here, we dismounted and our weary horses nibbled at the sparse grass while we sat on rocks and drank tea out of fine china cups. Clem leaned against a boulder and closed his eyes, apparently too exhausted to eat. We tourists took pictures of each other looking down at the chateau and the lake far, far below and congratulated ourselves for having made this amazing climb. I'm sure that arriving at the peak of Mount Everest could not generate any more pride and satisfaction than this ascent did for us. Some admitted having been quite terrified on the way up, however. And then we started to think about going down. For some reason, this seemed even more frightening. I could imagine us slipping and sliding down that impossibly narrow trail, crashing into each other and hurtling to the bottom in a broken tangle of horseflesh and humanity.

About this time, we noticed that Walt and Alison had disappeared into the teahouse. We heard them arguing inside.

"I won't do it," Alison sobbed. "You have to get me down another way. Get a helicopter or something."

"I'm sorry, lady," Walt replied. "There ain't no other way. I'll be right ahead of you. Don't worry. You'll be okay."

We looked at each other in amazement. Alison was afraid to go back down. In spite of her clothes and her know-it-all manner, she was the one who had chickened out. I think everyone else in the group felt even more proud of what we had done. It made us determined not to complain, but to go to our deaths with quiet dignity.

Moments on a Staircase

Secretly, I was grateful to Alison for her display of weakness. She had taken me off the hook. Now, no matter what happened, I would not be the worst one in the group. When it was time to go down the mountain my mind was at ease. If, by some miracle, we made it to the bottom in one piece, my reputation as a horsewoman would be intact. I woke Clem out of his reverie and climbed up on his bony back with a happy heart. The saddle was warm in the afternoon sun, so I took off my sweater and laid it across the pommel.

After much coaxing, Walt finally convinced Alison to get back on her horse and once again, he took the reins and led us down the trail. Our worst fears were confirmed as we scuffled and slid our way down the mountainside, feeling even less in control than we had on the way up. Imagine our horror when we saw another group of riders coming up the trail toward us. How would they get past? The trail was hardly wide enough for one horse, let alone two. We skidded along in silence as the group from below got closer and closer. Of course, there was room for two horses to pass, but one of them had to walk perilously close to the edge of the trail and it happened to be our group who moved over to the outside to let the others pass. I masked my fear and said, "Howdy," as they went by, secretly amused by their drawn faces and white knuckled grips on the reins. Just wait until you have to go down, I thought.

The new group had finally passed when their leader, farther up the trail, yelled down at us, "Did somebody lose a sweater?"

I reached for mine and, of course, it was gone.

"I did," I called out, "but never mind. It's an old one. I don't need it."

"Stay there," the voice called. "I'll bring it down to you."

"Oh, no. Don't bother," I shouted. But he had already turned his horse around and was heading back to me, threading his way expertly past the other riders in his group.

I pulled on my reins and Clem slid to a shuddering stop, but I could tell he didn't like the idea. He kept trying to start up again as we waited for the guy to come down to us. It took all my strength to hold him back as Kit and the last of our group passed us by.

Finally, the man reached my side and handed me my sweater. Then he told me to tie it to the saddle with some little leather thongs that were hanging there.

"It's okay," I said, but Mr. Helpful decided to show me how. He rolled my sweater into a neat bundle and fastened the ties around it carefully. Meanwhile, our group had travelled on quite a way and Clem was becoming very agitated, tossing his head and pawing at the ground with his hooves, sending little stones rattling down the trail. I had never seen him this animated. When at last the sweater was secure, I thanked the man, eased up on the reins and Clem began to move. Oh boy, did he move!

Our group had made several hair-pin turns by now and were quite far below on the trail. I remembered Walt's words of advice before we left the paddock: "Clem don't like to be last, so try to stay in the middle of the pack."

Oh God, Clem don't like to be last! But it was too late. Slipping and sliding, Clem scrambled down the trail and hit the first turn at a brisk canter. I was bouncing up and down in the saddle but, by some miracle, I stayed on.

When he rounded the turn and hit the straight of way, we were going at a full gallop. I don't remember much after that, but I know my mouth was wide open and I heard someone screaming.

Moments on a Staircase

I sawed at the reins, but by now Old Clem had the bit in his teeth and was not responding to anything but his wild, irrational urge not to be the last one in line.

As we began to catch up to our group, they stopped on the trail and stared up at us in wonder. At the last moment, they stepped aside in turn so Clem could pass. The boys waved and cheered and I saw Paul smiling proudly as I streaked by. Finally, in a cloud of dust and a hailstorm of loose rocks, we came to a halt near the centre of the group. Clem slowed to a walk, puffing and snorting from his efforts. As I sat shaking in my saddle, Kit rode up from behind, glaring sternly at me.

"Holy shit, lady. Are you one of those trick riders from the Stampede? I know you're good, but that was pretty damn foolish what you did," he said. "Even Walt and me, we don't gallop on this trail. It's amazing. I never seen anything like it. And we heard you yelling at poor old Clem trying to make him go even faster."

When we got back to the corral, and dismounted, my legs felt like jelly and I thought I was going to throw up. Clem looked at me with new respect in his big brown eyes. And the other members of the group stood in silent awe as I walked past them, bow-legged and wind-blown, to where my family was standing. The boys gazed at me with admiration shining from their eyes. "Jeez mom," they said proudly. "We didn't know you could ride like that. Great grandpa sure was right."

If only I had left well enough alone, I could have basked in the glory of that treacherous ride down the side of Mount Crumpet for the rest of my life. But I didn't. Oh no, not me! I started to believe the stories that circulated about my amazing feat of horsemanship.

Maybe it wasn't just a lucky coincidence I made it to the bottom of that mountain in one piece. Maybe I really had done what my husband and my children bragged about to anyone who would listen; guided a rogue stallion down the side of a mountain in the Rockies at a full gallop.

That's why, five years later, as my memory of what really happened faded and my fortieth birthday approached, I decided I wanted to take English riding lessons. I wanted to finally do it right; to ride like Walt and Kit, easy in the saddle, to look like Alison on the cover of *"Horse and Hound"*, to be a real equestrienne. And that's how I ended up in the clutches of the dreaded Ingrid, she of the doomsday whip.

After that first lesson, the disastrous up, down, up down, oomph, a normal person would have realized that some folks are just not cut out for the saddle. But if anything, I am determined, stubborn even, some might say. So I went back the next week for another try.

When I arrived for my second lesson that Saturday in May, I felt quite well turned out. I had purchased a black velvet riding helmet and new, knee length boots made of tooled leather. Ingrid looked at me approvingly and even the horses seemed impressed when I entered the barn in my new regalia. It was a signal to them that I meant business this time. No more oomphing around. The other members of the group seemed happy to see me and I was surprised and pleased that they remembered my name.

"Hi Mary," they said, grinning at me.

I was a bit embarrassed that I didn't remember their names until I thought about it. I certainly stood out from the crowd, being some thirty-odd years older than they were and it was my name that had been on Ingrid's lips every few minutes at our last meeting.

Moments on a Staircase

And how could they forget the sight of me crumpled up on the floor of the arena after my dismal failure to circumnavigate *'ze Vorld'*? No wonder they remembered me. But I was determined that things would be different this time around. I'd show them. This time I would do things right.

I had even been practising at home in secret. When no one was around, I would mount the end of the sofa which had big rounded arms, and I'd post up and down for hours, squeezing my thighs against the soft material and lowering myself gently. There were no oomphs from the sofa. After a few days I could feel the muscles of my legs getting stronger and my movements on the sofa getting better and better. One day my husband caught me in the middle of this exercise and he got excited at the thought of having a wife with nutcracker thighs.

Because the weather on this particular day was warm and sunny, Ingrid announced we would be riding in the outdoor arena. She took her customary place in the center and we formed a circle around her as the horses moved off at a brisk walk.

I had a different horse this time, a lanky brown gelding named Peter, so I felt like I was being given a second chance to prove myself. Hopefully the oomphing was the fault of that other horse and had nothing to do with me. Then Ingrid cracked her whip and shouted an order. "You vill trot please!"

I squeezed with my new, magic thighs and Peter lurched into a bouncy trot; up, down, up, down. This time there were no oomphs. I simply stayed up off the saddle, gripping with the powerful new muscles I had acquired from my practice on the sofa. I wasn't really posting, just sort of standing up in the stirrups while the horse moved beneath me. Unbeknownst to me, this was the position for cantering, so Peter, after a moment or two of confusion, began to stride along in this new mode. A canter is quite a bit faster than a trot, as any good horseman knows, so it was inevitable Peter would eventually run up on the hind end of the horse in front of us. The offended animal lashed out with its back legs, catching Peter on the nose with one of his hooves, causing him to rear up on his hind legs. Somehow, I remained upright in the stirrups hanging on grimly with my iron thighs.

"Stop!" Ingrid yelled. Crack! Crack!

"Mary, you vill please come into ze centre of ze ring!"

Oh no. I couldn't believe it. I had done it again. I could feel the hot tears welling in my eyes. I was a hopeless failure. I would never learn to post. I might as well give up my dream of becoming an equestrienne.

When Peter reached the spot where Ingrid was waiting she reached up and took hold of his bridle.

"Keep trotting mitt ze up and down," she said to the others.

Then she came close to the side of my horse and lowered her voice as she spoke just to me. "Mary, you have had *sax*?" she asked.

I didn't know what to say. I wasn't sure I had heard her properly.

"Huh?" I managed to croak.

"*Sax, sax,*" she whispered. "You are married mitt kinder, no?"

"Uh-uh," I said.

"Zen you must have had *sax*. Think about ze way you move ven you are making luff. Back and forth mitt ze loose hips and ze loosey-goosey back. Do you remember?"

"Yes, I remember," I said.

"Vell! Do it zen, like that. Not up and down, but more like in and out."

Back I went to the circle and Peter began to trot with the others. I tried to imagine that I was having 'sax' with the saddle. In, out, in, out. My God, it was working. I was posting just like the kids around me. Round and round we went until finally Ingrid ordered us to stop.

"Now you are doing it, Mary. Good for you," she said. "Did you enchoy it?" She laughed a wicked little laugh and went on with the lesson. I was deliriously happy.

"Now that everyone can trot, and Mary can even canter, ve vill proceed mitt ze chumping," Ingrid announced.

She laid a broom stick on the dirt and, one by one, we rode our horses up to it and they stepped over without missing a beat. All, that is, except Peter. We were trotting along nicely when he came to the stick lying in front of him and stopped dead in his tracks. I kept right on going. Up over the front of the saddle and down his neck I went until I was hanging on with both arms wrapped around him just beneath his head, with a mouth full of mane. Of course this added weight made his head bend down till his nose was resting just inches above the ground.

"Whoa, Peter, *mein schatze*," Ingrid cooed in a soothing voice.

She walked swiftly to stand by his head and take hold of the reins. Then slowly she encouraged him to raise his head, all the while talking softly and reassuringly to him. As his head went up, I slid back along his neck until I was sitting in front of the saddle.

"Get back in the saddle, Mary," Ingrid said quietly so as not to spook Peter.

This was not an easy task but, finally, with a great deal of squirming I managed to hoist myself back onto the proper side of the saddle. I felt great admiration for Ingrid's coolness under fire. If Peter had become frightened and tossed me off I might have broken my neck. I was amazed at the strength of the beast being able to hoist my great weight up in the air using just the muscles of his neck.

Jumping was suspended for the rest of the day and I was grateful to get down on dry land. I couldn't understand why Peter had decided to stop so abruptly when all the other horses had trotted over the broomstick without a flicker of fear. Ingrid came to the stall where I was brushing Peter.

"Why did he just stop like that for no reason?" I asked.

"You told him to stop," Ingrid said, matter-of-factly.

"No, I didn't," I said. "Why would I do that?"

"Oh, you didn't mean to do it. But you communicated it through the reins that you wanted him to stop. You have good hands, Mary. Zis I know. Your handling of the reins is very sensitive to the horse's mouth. He feels everything you are thinking ant ven you are afraid. Your hands told him to stop."

Oh, the injustice of it all. I had come so close to achieving my elusive goal of becoming an equestrienne, just to have it snatched away at the last moment. I had finally mastered the art of trotting by employing my new, erotic in and out moves, but now I was telegraphing subliminal messages to the horse's mouth with my hands. What was I supposed to do? Hold the reins in my teeth? Perhaps it was time to give up my dream.

I would bow out now while I still retained a small amount of dignity. No one need ever know about my ignominious failure.

"See you next week, Mary," Ingrid said.

"Yeah," I said, "see yuh."

How I wish I could end my equestrienne story differently; tell you I eventually learned to post and canter and gallop. That I became an accomplished jumper, sailing over fences and hedges like they do in English movies.

But the truth is, I mastered none of these feats. That doesn't mean I "fessed" up at home and let my family know. What was the point? Why disillusion them at this late date? I kept on with the weekly lessons for the rest of the summer because I enjoyed my little outings with my classmates, following along behind them on the trails, watching them gallop off into the sunset without me.

Ingrid finally gave up and left me alone to bring up the rear, strolling along at a leisurely walk. When we were in the arena, I walked in my own little circle in a corner of the large building so I wouldn't get in the way of the kids. They learned about changing leads and reversing directions and many other little niceties of horsemanship, while I steered my horse around piles of manure with the slightest touch of my ultra-sensitive hands. On the last day of class we had a picnic by the river and Ingrid offered me half of her sauerkraut sandwich.

"You haf done very vell for your age, Mary," she said. "But you should haf started earlier, ven you vas young. It vould haf been easier zen." Her voice was kind.

I didn't have the heart to tell her I had been at it since I was six.

This should have been the end of it. I had at last learned my lesson and accepted the fact that I would never become the rider

I had always dreamed of. But at least I had tried. Oh God, how I had tried!

And then, one day a few weeks later, when I came home from work, there was something standing in the corral at our hobby farm in Binbrook. It was big and brown and it had a large, blue bow attached to its bridle. It was a horse! And slowly it dawned on me that it was mine.

To celebrate my graduation from the riding academy, my dear husband had bought me a horse of my own. He had gone to an auction to buy a used tractor and came home with a real, live horse. His name was Justin and he was an eleven-year-old palomino gelding. He stood sixteen hands high and had a magnificent western saddle made of silver and tooled leather. Trigger never looked that good. Justin was everything I had ever dreamed of. But I was terrified. I had dodged many bullets in my equestrienne career, but this one, I knew, was too big to avoid. I had come to the end of the trail of lies and exaggeration I had been on for so many years.

My eyes filled with tears as I gazed at this magnificent beast. My family interpreted this as me being overwhelmed with joy.

"If anyone deserves a horse of their own, honey, it's you," my husband said proudly.

I'm sure he thought he had won first prize in the gift giving category for husbands. This wonderful, over-the-top present would make up for all the occasions when he had missed the mark in our twenty years of marriage. I didn't know what to say.

"Jump on and go for a ride, mom," the kids said. "He's all ready to go."

Moments on a Staircase

I made the excuse that I'd have to change into my riding togs first. "Why don't you guys take him out for a spin?" I suggested, hoping to delay the inevitable.

"No way," my husband interjected. "He's yours, so you get to be the first one to ride him. Hurry up and get dressed. We'll wait."

"Okay," I said, trying to sound excited at the prospect. But I knew it was just a matter of time before I was exposed as the impostor of the century.

On the way back down from my second floor bedroom I had a notion to fall down the stairs and pretend to be injured, but when I thought of my loving family waiting out there so excited to see me ride, I just couldn't do it.

I approached Justin and rubbed his nose, talking softly to him.

"Go easy on me, big fella," I said. Then I made sure he was up against the fence and I put my foot in the stirrup and swung up on his back. He stood patiently until I nudged my heels into his side and then he walked around the corral, as well-mannered and polite as you please, much to my relief. We went around several times without incident and I pulled him up in front of the spot where Paul and the boys were leaning on the fence..

"Make him go, mom," the kids said. "Let's see you gallop like you did at Lake Louise."

"Not today, guys. He's just new here. We don't want to spook him. Wait till he gets used to us. Let's take it slow." I could see they were disappointed.

"Can we ride him?" Ed asked.

"Sure," I said. "Just take it easy."

Jimmy changed places with me and Justin set off at a trot around the corral.

Up, down, up, down, Jimmy went, easy as you please. He looked completely at home as he moved rhythmically in time with the horse. At fifteen he was loose and supple in the saddle. I couldn't help smile to myself when I thought of all the times I had tried so hard to do what came so easy for him.

"My turn," Ed shouted as Jimmy brought Justin to a stop near us at the corral fence. Ed mounted up and Justin whirled away at a gallop. After one speedy circuit of the corral Ed headed him straight for the fence where we were standing. We scrambled for cover and watched in amazement as Justin soared effortlessly through the air and took off down the lane with Ed shouting, "yahoo", flapping his arms wildly.

I stood open-mouthed in disbelief. But Paul looked proudly after Ed and ruffled Jimmy's hair with his hand.

"Looks like we've got a couple of cowboys on our hands, Mary," he said. "Guess they take after their mother!"

Looking back, it was fun having a horse of my own, at first. I would come home from work, saddle Justin, and off we'd go down the lane, across the road to our neighbour's farm, along his lane and across a field to the creek at the back and into the woodlot that marked the edge of his two hundred acres. Les raised dairy cattle, black and white Holsteins, and if they happened to see us wandering by, they'd stop what they were doing, which was usually munching on something invisible, and follow us for a while.

It was beautiful in spring when the wildflowers decorated the banks of the creek and the hay was just starting to poke up out of the ground. It was equally glorious in the fall with the sun setting fire to the trees and Justin's feet kicking up leaves and sending them crackling. But I think winter was my favourite time of year. We would make fresh tracks in the new snow that was so clean and white it made me feel like Admiral Perry discovering the North Pole. Steam would rise from Justin's back and his breath would send puffs of smoke from his nostrils as we trekked along, all alone at the top of the world.

These idyllic moments didn't last very long, however. One day our neighbour Les came over for a visit. He gently hinted that we had left the gate to the pasture open when we passed through, and that the cows had followed us all the way up to the barn-- way early. They stood there bawling after we left, and Les had to milk them before their usual time just to shut them up. After that, it took about a week to get them back on their regular milking schedule. Who knew this about cows?

Another time, during one of his neighbourly chats, Les let it slip that we had walked across what had looked to me like an empty field, but was really a field of winter wheat just starting to poke up through the snow. We trampled quite a bit of it, apparently. After that, we stayed on our own property. We had twenty-five acres, nineteen of them rented out to Les, and the rest consisted of several pastures and an old orchard. Plenty of room to roam around on a horse.

I think Justin enjoyed our little jaunts. He would look up expectantly when I came into the stable to saddle him. It must have been a boring life alone all day with no other creatures around. We had no running water in the barn so it was necessary to carry pails of water from the house in winter or dip them out of the cistern by the barn bridge if it wasn't frozen over. I can remember frosty February mornings when Paul was on the night shift and I had to struggle alone out through the snow drifts to deliver water to Justin. He slurped it up greedily, demolishing two pails at one sitting. Then I'd open a bale of hay and stuff half of it into the manger with a few oats in the feed box for dessert. The process was repeated when I came home from school at supper time, and again before I went to bed. The boys were usually too busy to help.

"He's your horse, mom," they'd say, imitating what I'd often said to them in the past. *"It's your dog,"* or *"It's your kitten. You look after it."* Of course they didn't. Once in a while they took Justin out for a spin, but after a while the novelty wore off, and even these impromptu rides stopped happening. In their late teens, girls were infinitely more interesting than any horse.

Around this same time, I got a new job teaching primary gifted children and it required a great deal of extra work at home in the evenings. On the weekends I was too pooped to go riding. I could see that Justin was becoming depressed. He would lean on the fence and gaze at the house with a melancholy expression in his big brown eyes.

Then along came Harry. He was a white quarter horse that belonged to Ed's friend Lisa. It happened that she needed a place to board him and he ended up in our stable with Justin. The two geldings became fast friends and it was soon obvious that they loved each other very much. When Lisa came to take Harry out for a spin, Justin would trot along inside the pasture beside her until he ran out of room. Then he'd stand at the gate and watch as they headed down the lane, neighing anxiously until they came back. Harry did the same thing when Justin was out of his sight. They were most happy when Ed and Lisa rode together and they could trot along side by side, or when the two horses would stand nose to tail in the corral, swishing the flies off each other.

Harry was not only crazy about Justin, but he adored Lisa. When her little Volkswagen Bug came ripping down the lane, Harry would gallop over to the fence, whinnying and prancing with anticipation. Lisa had owned him since she was a little girl and they had taken many prizes at the local fall fairs for barrel racing. Lisa was the expert rider I had always dreamed of being. When she and Harry galloped off through the fields she stuck to his back like a burr. It was as if they were one entity. After a ride Lisa would walk around the barnyard with Harry following her like a pet dog.

Sometimes Lisa would lie down on the grass on our front lawn and Harry would lie beside her. She'd lean back against his side and fold her hands behind her head. They were the picture of contentment and mutual affection.

How I wish I could say that Justin and I had formed such an attachment over the years. But for some reason it just didn't happen. He never lost that far-away look in his eyes which I interpreted as a longing for the girl who had owned him before Paul bought him at auction that day. Apparently, Justin had made quite a fuss being loaded into the trailer and the girl had been in tears saying good-bye to him. I don't think Justin ever got over missing her.

That's why, after the boys left home and we sold the farm, we gave Justin to the young girl next door. I could see Justin's ears perk up when she came with her father to get him. She was a sweet young thing and talked softly to Justin as she rubbed his nose. The girl likely reminded him of his first owner, and he seemed happy to go with her. He trotted jauntily off down the lane, without so much as a backward glance at us, his family for nine years.

At last, my life of pretense and self-delusion was over. I was in my late fifties, feeling the early twinges of arthritis and I knew with certainty I would never be an equestrienne. But that was not the end. Not quite yet.

Many years later, my son Ed, married by now, with a young daughter named Sammie, came to pick me up at my apartment.

"Where are we going?" I asked.

"I have a surprise for you, mom," he said.

We drove out to the country to a farm in Ancaster. Rolling Meadows was the name on the sign out front, but I was not fooled. It was Jack Mellow's Riding Academy, the scene of my earliest equestrienne disasters.

"What are we doing here? I asked.

"Just wait and see," Ed replied.

He led me through the open doors into the stable where a few little girls were grooming their horses. We walked into the riding area and there, in the middle of the arena, stood a familiar figure. She was older, a little thicker around the middle, but still straight as a storm trooper in her knee-high leather boots, riding crop at the ready. It was Ingrid Kohn and facing her in a semi-circle were eight horses and eight little girls in hard helmets, listening earnestly as Ingrid spoke.

"You vill valk in a circle, facing zis way," she said, pointing with her whip. "Ant you vill squeeze mitt your legs ant ze horse vill trot. Up, down, up, down, up down. Off you go." Crack!

One of the little girls waved from her perch atop a large black horse. I looked closely. It was my granddaughter Sammie. Then she turned her horse into the circle and began to trot. She seemed to float effortlessly on the saddle, moving with ease around the arena. As she passed the place where we were standing she smiled at us, a look of pure joy on her face. It was a beautiful sight. At that moment I realized that somehow, in some mysterious way, my lifelong dream had come true.

"Takes after her grandma," Ed said.

Chapter 12 - Beware of Greeks

In 2001, after forty-three exciting years of marriage, Paul died suddenly and unexpectedly on June 7th, his birthday. That morning I had wished him happy birthday as he sat at the table drinking his coffee and reading the paper. I was heading out to work at our son Jim's greenhouse business, Cottage Pottage. I leaned over Paul and said, "Give me a kiss, I'm on my way."

He pecked me on the cheek, hardly taking his eyes off the story he was reading.

"So long, Mare. Have a nice day," he said

I planted my elbow on the newspaper, looking right into those gorgeous blue eyes.

"Hey, you're only sixty-eight! You can do better than that."

"Stick around and I'll show you," he said.

"Later, honey. You don't get your birthday present 'till tonight."

He laughed and kissed me on the lips, then pushed me away from his precious sports page. It was the last time I saw him alive.

Moments on a Staircase

The next time I saw him, he was lying on a gurney in the basement of the Dunnville hospital. To my horror, his eyes opened slowly as he lay there. Instead of the warm, challenging look I was used to, I saw beautiful, glittering blue orbs completely devoid of life. There was no question; he was dead.

I took his hand and rubbed it on my face, up and down on my cheek, memorizing the familiar touch on my skin, burning that feeling into my brain. I knew I would never feel that hand again. I didn't cry. Not then. I was too numb.

After the funeral, friends and relatives gradually drifted away, the cards stopped filling my mailbox every day and all the flowers died. I was left alone.

I was glad to be alone. I was dead, too, but nobody knew it. I didn't want to go anywhere or do anything with anybody. My life was over. I wanted to go to sleep and never wake up again. Maybe then, the incredible pain gnawing away at my mid-section would go away.

During this time, one person persisted in trying to get me out of my misery, my old friend Lou. We had been friends since high school, an astonishing fifty years ago. She was divorced and recently retired from her nursing career. And she just wouldn't leave me alone.

"Come on, let's go to the movies," she'd say.

"No thanks. I have a headache."

"Get your sweater and I'll start the car."

"I told you, I don't want to go out. I have a headache."

"You never have headaches. Here's a Tylenol, take this."

"Stop playing Nurse Jane Fuzzy-Wuzzy with me. I'm not going."

"Don't forget to lock the door."

Lou was nothing if not stubborn. I went to the movies. And surprisingly, the pain in my gut subsided for a while as I got lost in the story. It was *The Notebook*, Nicholas Sparks' tale of a love that lasted many years and ended with the heroine mired in the murky depths of Alzheimer's. In the last scene, the couple were in bed, locked in each others' arms and blissfully dead. The audience wept unashamedly all around us.

Not me.

I thought how glad I would have been to die in Paul's familiar embrace. We should be cheering this happy ending, I thought as I clapped loudly. Lou hustled me out of the theatre smiling apologetically at the other patrons.

But she didn't give up. Not Lou. She kept at it for a year.

"Remember when our group of girlfriends graduated from high school, how we made a pledge to go on a trip when we all retired?" Lou said.

"Yeah, what did we know? We were crazy back then."

"Well, guess what. I'm the last one to retire and I've been talking to some of the gang and they want to go. Whadda you say?"

"Hasta la vista, baby!"

"Come on, Mary. Don't be a stick-in-the-mud. You made a sacred promise. You've got to live up to it."

"Where are you going, Buffalo?"

"No, smarty. Audrey wants to go to Greece. She went before and loved it."

"How will you get there?"

"On an airplane. Olympic Airways flies non-stop from Toronto to Athens. We're going in September. It's cheaper at that time of year. It'll only cost around eight hundred dollars. Are you game?"

"Are you nuts?"

"Get your suitcase out and start packing. You're coming."

"I'm afraid to fly. I only flew once, to London and it was awful. I was scared shitless."

"I have some meds for you. You won't feel a thing."

"No, absolutely not. I have no desire to go to Greece. It's too far away and it's full of foreigners. Be sure to send me a postcard from the Parthenon."

On the day of the trip I waited, face like a thundercloud, for the airport limo. I didn't want to go. Why did I let that little gadfly talk me into things I didn't want to do? Well, it was too late now. I had to go, but I wasn't going to have a good time. That much I was sure of.

Three of us boarded the plane that day in September; Lou, Audrey, and me. The other girls had backed out of their 'sacred pledge.'

Audrey had invited her cousin Betty to join us. She loved to travel and had been recruited by Audrey to make an even number. Betty usually liked to travel alone, but she made an exception this time. She was very well organized and planned every day down to the last detail. Lou and Audrey went along with her ideas and I didn't care. I just wanted to get it over with and get back home to wrap myself in my cocoon of self-pity.

Moments on a Staircase

We arrived in Greece on a lovely, sunny day. Betty hailed a taxi and we were whisked away from the airport in Piraeus to the Royal Olympic Hotel in Athens.

"When we're unpacked we'll go to the Plaka for lunch," Betty announced.

I flopped on my bed in the room Lou and I were to share and closed my eyes.

"What the hell is a Plaka?" I said.

I found out it was an ancient market district close to our hotel, so we walked. As we ventured further into the labyrinth of narrow, winding streets, we were accosted at every turn by little shops full of local wares; jewellery, paintings, ceramics and clothing. You name it, they sold it here. I started to become interested in the incredible variety of goods displayed in the windows of the shops. Then I made the mistake of stopping to admire a T-shirt hanging on a rack outside one of the stores. The shopkeeper came out, sidled up to me, very close, and whispered in my ear.

"For you, beautiful lady, only ten euros." He looked like Anthony Quinn in *Zorba the Greek*. I was surprised.

"No thanks," I said, moving away from him. This was not the kind of attention I usually got from men.

"Come inside," he coaxed in a soft voice. "I have other things in here to show you."

"No, I don't really want a shirt. I was just looking."

"You have good taste, beautiful lady. Nine euros, for your good taste." He looked me up and down, smiling.

"Thanks, but I don't want anything today."

"Only seven euros, because of your lovely hair." He reached out to touch my head. With his other hand he conveniently barred my way out between the racks of shirts.

I drew myself up to my full height and looked him in the eye.

"Excuse me," I said, in my best school teacher voice.

"Of course, beautiful lady", he said, bowing slightly and moving aside as he spoke. "Where is your hotel? I will bring the shirt to you tonight. Is this the one you like? Only five euros, just because you are so lovely."

I ducked out of his reach and hurried back to the other girls. They were laughing at my obvious embarrassment.

"I told you to beware of Greeks bearing gifts," Betty said.

At lunchtime we ate at a little café under the trees. There were several tables in the dappled shade. I was surprised to see that the checked tablecloths were covered by clear plastic sheets. A waiter appeared quickly from the doorway of a nearby restaurant. He went around the table and took our orders for drinks. He seemed friendly asking each of the girls if they were married. Audrey said yes. Betty said no, she had never been married and Lou informed him that she was divorced. When he got to me, he leaned over and spoke softly into my ear.

"Are you married?" he asked.

"No," I said. "I'm a widow." He bent closer until I felt his breath warm on my neck.

"I have a nephew named Andreas," he said. "He will marry you. He has never been in jail. You will love him."

I saw the other girls looking at me with their mouths open so I decided to play along, just for laughs.

"Hmmm," I said. "How old is this nephew of yours?"

"Thirty-five. He is very good-looking. All the girls love him."

At this point he took a cell phone from his pocket.

"If you say yes, I will call him. He will come right over here to see you. You will love him, I know." He stared at me earnestly, fingers poised over the keypad of his phone. I started to feel bad that I was stringing him along.

"I'm sure he's very nice," I said, "but he's a bit too old for me. Thanks anyway."

He looked crestfallen as he slid the cell phone back into his pocket.

"What will you have to drink madame?" he said.

Betty ordered for us. The food was fantastic, a true Greek salad topped with a large slice of feta cheese and some tiny fried fishes complete with their fricasseed eyeballs staring up at us. This was topped off with a carafe of red wine which we shared. After a few glasses, I found myself gesturing with the little fish in my fingers as I talked. Then, without any qualms I popped it into my mouth. When we were finished, our waiter came to the table with the bill and in one seamless motion gathered up the corners of the plastic tablecloth and carted it off inside, dishes, salt and pepper and all. He made a point of not looking at me. I was glad, because I was beginning to be uncomfortable with all this attention.

Later in the hotel room, I stared into the mirror. Beautiful lady? Are you kidding? I was sixty-two years old and looked it. My 'lovely hair' was newly streaked with blond highlights to cover the encroaching gray. But there was no covering up the wrinkles around my eyes and the lines that bracketed my mouth. Lou caught me.

"Hey, gorgeous. What are you looking at?" she said.

"Why did the shopkeeper pick on me? And the waiter?" I asked. "What kind of vibe do I give off that made him think I'd be a match for his thirty-five-year old nephew? What kind of a crazy place is this?"

"I don't know, but don't fight it. Just go with the flow."

I noticed something else as I studied my reflection. There was a definite glow about me. My cheeks were pink from all this flattery and attention, and my eyes looked alive for the first time in a long while. I had to admit, a part of me had enjoyed playing the game. I didn't know it then, but I had taken my first step toward accepting that infamous Greek gift of the Trojan horse.

That night Audrey made a reservation at her favourite rooftop restaurant overlooking the Acropolis. The tables were set under the stars that hung just out of reach in a blue velvet sky. The Parthenon's white marble gleamed as the soft glow of moonlight illuminated its perfect proportions. It was magic.

"What a beautiful sight," I said.

"You are also a beautiful sight, madame." The voice in my ear belonged to our maitre d', who inhaled a deep breath through his prominent nose. "Your perfume is intoxicating," he whispered.

"Eforestow", I said, reading the Greek for thank you from the translations provided on the back of the wine list.

"Madame is Greek?" The waiter could hardly contain his excitement. "I knew it."

Moments on a Staircase

"Take it easy, Mary." Betty put her hand on my arm. "Give him an inch and he'll take a mile." She made a shooing motion with her other hand and he scurried away.

"Yiassou," I called after him.

I started not to like Betty. She was bossy and overbearing. I could look after myself without any help from her. When she announced that later on we were going to a concert by the Chinese national orchestra in the ancient theatre in Athens, I dug in my heels and said, "No thanks. I want to see some real Greeks out having fun."

Three of us said goodbye to Betty and piled into a taxi.

"Where do Athenians go for fun?" I asked our driver who said his name was Dimitri.

"I will take you to a wonderful place," he said. "It belongs to my cousin, George. Are you ladies married?"

What was this Greek obsession with marriage? I wondered. I decided to cut him off at the pass.

"What about you, Dimitri, are you married?"

His normally pleasant expression twisted into a nasty snarl.

"Greek women are shit," he said.

The taxi took off and made a u-turn in the middle of the street. Now we were headed for the waterfront district. Left and right, back and forth, Dimitri guided the old Mercedes through the dark, narrow streets. After a few anxious moments, we arrived at a well-lit building full of people and music. There was nowhere to park, so Dimitri pulled the car up on the sidewalk. George came out of the restaurant when Dimitri called to him and he explained that they were celebrating a christening.

Moments on a Staircase

From somewhere inside a baby was crying. Bouzouki music could be heard playing in the inner room and people were dancing enthusiastically, some kind of Greek folk dance, arms linked in a large circle. We sat at the outdoor patio near the open doors and watched. These were real Greek people, a large boisterous family group, and we were the only tourists to be seen. One of the men asked Lou to dance and away she went. Lou had never said no to a dance invitation in her life. Someone handed her a kerchief and her little five-foot body became lost on the crowded dance floor. Only her twirling scarf let us know that she was still there in the middle of the scrum. Audrey and I drank quite a few shots of raki, a strong red liqueur, before we realized we were becoming tipsy. At last, Lou came back, panting and laughing. "Opa," she giggled as she dropped into a chair.

Later, things quieted down a bit and the music turned slow and romantic. A thirty-ish woman came to stand in the middle of the room. She was joined by a man who knelt before her on one knee. The woman offered him the end of her scarf, which he took in his hand. Then she danced around him, hips swaying provocatively as he gazed at her, never taking his eyes off her suggestive movements. I felt we shouldn't be watching this intimate dance. When they were done, the couple kissed and embraced and the other people surrounded them applauding. Dimitri explained that this was the mother and father of the child who had been christened. If this was Greek foreplay, I imagined there might be more christenings for them in the future.

A large vehicle lumbered down the street and began towing a car that was illegally parked. Dimitri quickly herded us into the Mercedes. Back at the hotel, Audrey and I tottered down the long hallway leading to our rooms as Lou skipped along beside us waving her scarf. On the way we passed several replicas of famous Greek statues displayed in niches. The one on guard outside our door was an athletic young man, muscles and sinews prominent on his naked body. Audrey said it was The Discus Thrower. Lou and I giggled like school girls as we ran our hands over his marble perfection.

It had been a memorable evening. When we told Betty about it, she said we had missed a wonderful concert by the Chinese orchestra. We could tell she was miffed.

"The acoustics were marvellous," she said. "And they played my favourite Mahler symphony."

Somehow, I doubted that Mahler could compare to a bunch of energetic Greeks doing the *Sirtaki*.

As I lay in bed, I thought about what had transpired that day. I was totally confused. Apparently I was a fatal attraction to Greek waiters and shop keepers, for some reason. Despite what they said, I knew I wasn't beautiful. Why did they hit on only me?

It seemed important that I was a widow. That was the only difference I could think of. But why was that so interesting to them? Would Andreas really have married me if I'd taken the bait? These thoughts raced through my head as I drifted off to sleep. In my dreams, the Discus Thrower was making love to me and I was powerless to resist his stony advances.

As I woke up slowly, I realized that I hadn't thought once about wanting to die, and the pain in my solar plexus had diminished significantly. It all came back to me as a mantle of guilt fell over my thoughts. Some grieving widow I was.

Next morning, I checked in the mirror again. It was still there, the face that launched a thousand ships; rosy cheeks, shining eyes and all. I was so spoiled by all the attention I had been getting that I was slightly disappointed to find breakfast was a buffet affair--not a waiter in sight.

Moments on a Staircase

But my disappointment was soon forgotten when I stepped onto the tour bus that was to take us on a four-day trip around the Peloponnese.

"*Yiassou,*" I said, as I climbed up the steps of the bus, smiling at the lanky, middle-aged man sitting in the driver's seat.

"*Yiassas,*" he replied, his face lighting up with a wide grin. When I got to the top step he said, "You are *kookla.*"

I turned to the tour guide who was standing beside him. "Did he just say I was crazy?"

"No, no," she laughed. "He said you are very beautiful, like a doll. *Kookla* means doll." Then she turned to him. "Behave yourself, Stathis."

"But where did you get all these *kooklas*?" he asked as Audrey and Lou followed me onto the bus.

Lou and I sat directly behind the driver across the aisle from Audrey and Betty. We were all laughing about me thinking he said we were crazy.

"If only he knew," Betty said.

During the ride out of Athens our guide, Joanna, pointed out the sights as we passed. Occasionally, when I looked away from our window, I noticed that I had a clear view of the rear-view mirror attached to the large windshield of the bus. Reflected in it were the driver's mischievous brown eyes set in a tanned, pleasant face. They seemed to be staring at me. Could he see me as plainly as I saw him? I smiled at the mirror and immediately he smiled back. That answered my question. Throughout the morning I felt his eyes on me many times. After lunch, I asked Lou to trade places but she wanted to stay in the window seat. I didn't tell her that I was starting to feel uncomfortable with all this scrutiny from the driver. But more importantly, I wondered who was watching the road while he stared at me.

The bus lumbered down the highway and then off onto a dirt road heading out into the hilly countryside. Soon we were at the Lion's Gate that guarded the ancient city of Mycenae. When we got off the bus, Stathis, who was stationed at the bottom step, extended his hand to help the passengers down. As I alighted from the last step, I felt his fingers close around mine tightly, and when I tried to move away from him, I found myself held captive in his strong grip. With his free hand he pointed to the little Canadian flag I wore on my t-shirt.

"*Canadesa.*" He smiled approvingly at me as the other tourists behind me waited impatiently to leave the bus.

"*Ne,*" I said, remembering the Greek for *yes* from the wine list.

He spoke to Joanna in Greek and laughed as she frowned and gave him a playful shove. I moved away as soon as I could retrieve my hand. What did he say about me? And why had he picked me out from the crowd of tourists, mostly female and much younger and more attractive than me. I began to feel like a wounded gazelle trailing behind the herd while the lions gathered in the grass ready to spring. Why me, Lord, why me?

When we stopped for coffee at a little outdoor taverna near the Corinth Canal, I saw Stathis watching me from the bar where he and Joanna were sitting. Whenever he caught my eye, he winked and smiled suggestively at me. I turned away hoping he would take the hint. By now, the other passengers of the bus were beginning to notice and stared at me when I walked by. I was becoming notorious, some kind of *femme fatale*. My own travelling companions thought it was funny.

"You sure are getting the once over, Mary," Lou laughed.

"Yeah, what are you doing to that poor guy?" Audrey chimed in.

"I don't think it's wise to flirt with him," Betty said. "You might be sorry."

"I'm not doing anything," I said. "It's like I have a sign on my back that says 'Desperate Widow'"

Joanna must have seen my distress. She approached me on our way out and said, "Don't be upset, Mary. Stathis is a nice guy. He just gets lonely on these long trips. And he feels responsible for you in a funny way. Here we believe there is a special place in hell for a man who won't sleep with a woman who needs sex. Greek men think widows can't live without it, so they are fair game."

That night at our hotel in Nauplia, I tried to avoid Stathis whenever possible. I noticed him in the bar drinking with some other tour bus drivers, so I headed the other way to the swimming pool.

The other girls had declined to go with me, so I had time to think about what I had learned today. It was a relief to know I wasn't giving off some kind of pheromone that made me an easy target for the attention I was receiving from men. Joanna had said it was a cultural thing. When I thought about it, it made sense in a strange way. Women like Audrey, with husbands at home, were off limits. A divorcee like Lou might have a lot of baggage. And an old maid like Betty wasn't worth all that effort. That left widows like me, lonely and desperate for male companionship.

I had to admit that I did miss the intimacy of marriage, lying warm and satisfied in Paul's arms while he fell asleep breathing softly into my hair. I longed to feel that way again, but I knew it could never be. My love life was over. I guess I'd have to be satisfied with dreaming about a man made of marble.

When I went back to the room to get dressed, Lou wasn't there. She left a note that she and the other girls had gone to the pub in the hotel and I should meet them there. Then I made a fatal mistake. I put on a pair of white pants and a cute blue shirt I had picked up in the Plaka. The colour of the shirt was quite unusual, a bright cerulean blue, like the colour of the Aegean Sea. I headed down to the pub looking quite snazzy, I thought, but I was not prepared for the reception I got.

When I walked in, a table of drivers and guides near the door all stopped talking and stared at me. They rose, as one, from their chairs and applauded, smiling as I went by. I was horrified. What the hell had I done now?

Once again, Joanna came to my rescue. "Mary, you are wearing the exact colours of the Greek flag. That's why they're clapping for you. Greeks are very patriotic, you know. We have lived under the rule of many conquerors who didn't allow us to fly a Greek flag. We paint our houses white and the doors and shutters this shade of blue, just like the flag." She indicated my shirt.

" So, I am a walking, talking Greek flag," I said. I looked at Stathis who was beaming at me with a proprietary look in his eyes. Oh God, I had aroused his passion for me even more by wearing this outfit.

Late in the evening, after too many ouzos to count, Stathis came to the table of women who were left in the pub. Betty had gone to bed, and Audrey went with her. Lou and I were left with a group of four American girls. He sat across from me and stared lovingly into my eyes.

Moments on a Staircase

"Hey Stathis," one of the Americans said, "How do you feel sitting here with all these women? You are a lucky man."

"Yas," he said, "but you know the one I want."

His gaze almost burned a hole in me. I didn't know where to look. I got up from the table and mumbled something to Lou about going to bed and started to leave. As I passed his chair, Stathis reached out and took my hand for a moment. When I left, I felt something in my palm. It was a note that read, Room 233.

I showed it to Lou when she came back from the pub.

"Why don't you go?" she said.

"I'm not going to some strange man's room for sex."

"Why not? You might have fun. I noticed he has big feet." I went to bed not speaking to her.

Next morning when we boarded the bus, Stathis had a pained expression on his face.

"Why you not come?" he said as I slid into my seat.

"I'm sorry," I said. "I don't do things like that."

Stathis started up the bus and we careened out of the parking lot and onto the highway. It was silent at the front of the bus, no joking or kidding around with Joanna. He was obviously miserable. When we turned off the highway into the mountains on the way to Delphi, Stathis drove like a madman, speeding around hairpin turns as though the devil were after him. When we reached the sacred site, everyone was glad to get off the bus. As I passed him, Stathis looked at me with pleading eyes.

"You will come to me tonight?" he said

I was glad when Joanna intervened again. "Now Stathis," she said firmly, "be a good boy."

Lou told me several members of the tour spoke to her in private. "Tell your friend to go with him," they said. "Please. Or we will never get out of here alive."

I was horrified that the whole bus was involved in this sordid little affair. I wanted it to end, but decided the only way that would happen was if I talked to him in private. I would let him know in a kind way that I was not up for grabs. So that night, after he had slipped me his room number again, I found myself knocking on his door around nine o'clock. Lou promised she would come and get me if I wasn't back in half an hour.

It all seemed very cloak and dagger and, I must admit, exciting. My heart was beating rapidly as I waited for him to open the door.

I was rehearsing what I would say when it flew open and I was wrapped in a pair of long, strong arms.

"*Amorphoso,*" Stathis murmured into my ear. "*Sagapo.*"

These were not words I recognized, but they sounded like insults somehow. I knew amorphous meant shapeless, and saggy was a shape I was becoming familiar with.

I struggled in his embrace but this only served to make him bolder. Next thing I knew, I was on my back on his bed and he was tugging at one of my knee length boots. I put my foot on his chest and shoved with all my might. To my surprise he reeled backwards into the closed drapes and for a moment he disappeared. When he came out of his drapery cocoon, I got a glimpse of a wide-open window behind him leading to a cement courtyard two stories below. By some miracle, he had held on to the curtain long enough to stop himself from hurtling backwards to his death. To his credit, he didn't lose hold of my boot.

"Stop it!" I yelled.

He stood looking down at me, breathing hard, then turned away and sat down on a nearby chair. I scrambled to my feet, grabbed my boot and made my way to the door.

"Please don't bother me any more, Stathis. You are a nice man, but I'm not looking for one right now. Thank you, but no thanks." I made as dignified a retreat as possible given I only had one boot on and my hair and clothes were in disarray.

For the rest of the trip, Stathis was quiet and subdued. When we said goodbye, he held my hand for a long moment then raised it to his lips and kissed it. When I looked, a paper had magically appeared in my hand. On it he had written a phone number.

"*Yiassas.*" he said, hopefully.

I felt really bad about what I had done to him. But I made the excuse that I couldn't help it. I hadn't encouraged him, although somewhere in the corner of my mind I had to admit that I had enjoyed being the centre of attention for once. The girl who had spent her school days as a wallflower had magically become the belle of the ball in a country half a world away. I thought I knew how Helen of Troy must have felt.

As we entered the hotel through the big glass front doors, Betty brought me back to earth with her own explanation of events.

"I know why all those Greek waiters and the bus driver were after Mary," she said.

Moments on a Staircase

The three of us waited expectantly. Betty walked over to a large statue in the lobby. It was Athena in full armour, complete with her unfeminine features and masculine proportions.

"Mary looks just like Athena," Betty announced.

The next day I looked up the unfamiliar words I had heard in my brief encounter with Stathis in his room. According to my dictionary, *Amorphoso* meant 'beautiful' and *Sagapo,* in Greek, meant 'I love you'.

Later, when I got back home to my life of loneliness and misery, I thought about what I might have missed. I had shut the door on a man who professed to love me and thought I was beautiful. What was the matter with me? I went back to Greece alone in November that same year. I was sure Paul would have cheered me on. I felt that I owed it to him to live life to the max. I had seen first hand how quickly it can all be over.

I called the number Stathis had pressed into my hand and he answered immediately.

"Hi Stathis," I said, "it's Mary from Canada. Do you remember me?"

There was a long silence and then I heard his voice.

"Yas, yas, I remember. The kookla. Where are you?"

"I'm here...in Athens...at the Hotel Arethusa. I came back to see you."

I heard him laughing at the other end of the line. "You came all the way back to see me? I don't believe. Stay right where you are. I will come and get you. You are make me very happy today, Mary."

Moments on a Staircase

I was relieved to hear how excited he sounded. But then I started to worry. He would expect me to have sex with him. I didn't know if I could do it. I wasn't sure if I could remember all the steps to the mating dance. Besides, I had never been a very good dancer.

I checked myself out in the mirror before he came. Yes, there it was, that magic inner glow lighting up my ordinary features and making me look almost beautiful. I hoped I wouldn't disappoint him.

By the look on his face when I stepped out of the elevator in the lobby, I needn't have worried. He was obviously happy to see me and greeted me with a warm hug.

"Yiassas, Mary," he said. "I am not believe you came back to me. Why you come now but not before?"

"I wasn't ready then," I said.

"But now? You are ready now?"

I could feel myself blushing hotly as he took my hand and raised it to his lips.

"Ne," I said.

We walked across the street to the National Gardens where we sat on a bench in the sunlight. Ducks swam in a pond nearby and lovers strolled arm in arm along the paths under the trees. Stathis took my hand and gently guided it to his lap. I felt the hard, swollen flesh through his clothing.

"See what you do to me?" he murmured in my ear as his lips brushed my cheek. I was embarrassed, hoping no one had seen this. But I was also intrigued by his boldness. Obviously he didn't pussyfoot around. He knew what he wanted and wasn't afraid to go for it.

Moments on a Staircase

We left the park and found his car, which he had stashed at the back of the hotel after paying the man at the front desk a few euros. Parking in Athens, I remembered, was practically non-existent. The car was an antique Chevy sedan that Stathis informed me he was refurbishing. It shone in all its blue metallic glory in the hot Greek sunlight. I felt quite comfortable in the soft leather seat beside him as we threaded our way through the traffic to the main highway leading out of the city.

"Where are we going?" I asked

"I am surprise you, Mary," he said. "I think you will like it. It is long away from here. Do you mind if I scoot?"

For a moment I felt my built in Canadian reserve taking over my thoughts. What the hell was I doing in this old car with a man I didn't know going God knows where in a strange country? Then I remembered how suddenly life can be over and all its surprises gone forever. I put my fears away. I liked this guy and he had never made me feel unsafe. Why not take a chance and see what happens. I had come a long way and I might never have this opportunity again.

"Go ahead, Stathis. Scoot," I said.

Immediately he bore down on the gas a pedal and the big car rocketed along the highway. Stathis opened the window and warm air rushed in as he sang in a loud voice along with a Greek song on the radio. He reached over and placed my hand on the smooth, burled walnut knob of the gearshift, covering my fingers with his palm. He steered with the other hand on the wheel. It was like a crazy, midway ride at the fair.

At last we pulled off the road and took a little detour through the main street of a small town by the water. Stathis seemed to know all the people we passed, yelling at them and waving out the window. Finally, we parked in front of a taverna right on the waterfront. We sat at a small table for two and Stathis ordered lunch. It was some kind of eggplant dish with french-fries on the side. We shared a bottle of red wine. Every so often Stathis would put his arm around me and kiss my cheek.

"You have beautiful eyes," he said. "Like . . . *gata*. Can you see in the dark with those eyes?"

I can't remember what we talked about but I do recall feeling warm and desirable and happy for the first time in a long time.

After lunch, Stathis showed me his new cell phone. He wanted to show it off so he asked me to tell him someone in Canada he could call. I said, "My sister, Barbara. She'll get a kick out of it."

He pressed a few buttons and in a few moments I heard my sister's surprised voice.

"Hello. Mary? Is that you?"

"Hello Varvara," Stathis answered. "I am Stathis Marinakas. I am here in Greece with your sister. How are you?"

They chatted for several minutes. My sister never met anyone she couldn't talk to.

After lunch we continued on our journey, ending up a few hours later in a little town he called Loutraki. It was dark by the time we arrived. The main attraction, a large casino, was lit up like a Christmas tree. Stathis was obviously excited as he practically galloped into the place, dragging me along behind him. I left him at the roulette table and went to play the slot machines nearby. Every once in a while, I looked over at him. After a while I noticed a large pile of chips in front of him. He caught my eye and winked, smiling broadly and gesturing at his winnings. I was starting to get hungry, but I had enough sense to leave him alone. I had seen that glitter in Paul's eyes once, when he was shooting craps with his firehouse buddies at a party. When I tried to drag him away before he lost his money, he had resisted vehemently. I waited patiently for Stathis to come and find me in the restaurant area. When he showed up he had cashed in his chips and come away with eight hundred euros in his pocket. I could only imagine what a huge sum this must have been to him. Needless to say he was very happy.

"Did you win any money, Mary?" he asked.

When I said I had lost, he asked me how much and proudly handed me forty euros.

"For my lucky charm," he said.

On the way home Stathis produced a bottle of wine from under the seat of the car, and we passed it back and forth, swigging and singing our way along the deserted highway back to Athens. By the time we got to the Hotel Arethusa, I was feeling no pain.

Stathis bargained with the desk clerk, once again, and managed to find a place to park the car while I went up to the room alone. When I got there, I had a moment of doubt about what I was about to do. How could I betray Paul this way? He was the love of my life. I had been true to him for forty-three years. I didn't love Stathis. I didn't really even know him. What the hell was I thinking? By the time he knocked on the door of my room I had decided to tell him I had changed my mind. I hoped he would understand and not be as upset as the last time I had rejected his advances.

But I didn't have a chance to tell him I had chickened out. He swept into the room and threw his arms around me, kissing me and caressing me enthusiastically. When I tried to turn away, he was there, his lips capturing mine before I could speak. His hands were everywhere; my back, my breasts, my thighs. I began to think he was an octopus.

"No, no, no," I blurted out each time my lips were free of his kisses. But this only seemed to make him more ardent. Then I remembered that *ne* meant yes in Greek. He probably thought I was saying, *yes, yes, yes*. I gave up the struggle.

Next thing I knew I was naked in bed looking up at him. He knelt over me gazing as though he were admiring a Rubens painting.

"Amorphoso," he muttered over and over again as his hands cupped my breasts and he bent to kiss them.

I felt heat building up inside me as he touched me gently, firmly, in places that hadn't been touched for over two years. He licked my earlobes, my eyes, my thighs, my knees. His tongue even traced the path of my gallbladder scar as it carved its way across my mid-section. I stopped all my evasive tactics. It was no use. He was a veritable Scarlet Pimpernel of erotic activity. He was here, he was there, he was everywhere at once.

Through a wine-soaked haze I let myself feel it all. Paul couldn't feel anything anymore and I might never have a chance to feel this way again. I let go of all my inhibitions and held on to Stathis with all my might. It was a wild ride.

I don't know how long it lasted. It seemed like forever, but when it was over and we were lying side by side in a sweaty heap, I started to cry.

"Why you crying, Mary? Did I hurt you?" He seemed genuinely concerned as he patted my shoulder.

"No, you didn't hurt me, Stathis. Don't worry," I said.

Then he smiled tenderly at me. "This is the first time since your husband died?"

"Yes," I said, through my tears.

"Don't worry," he said. "He loved you, and I love you, too. He would want you should be happy. I make you happy?"

"Yes, Stathis. You make me happy. I didn't think anyone could make me feel this way again, but you did. Thank you."

"I will come to Canada to visit you. At Christmas time. You have Christmas in Canada?" he asked.

"Yes, we do. That would be nice."

Before he left that night, we made plans to meet again the next day. He wanted to take me to Lycavitos Hill. We went up in a little funicular and got out at the top of the hill. An old derelict was sitting beside the door of the church perched on top of the hill, and Stathis went over and gave him some money.

"Do you know him?" I asked.

"No, but he is an old freedom fighter from the war. I like to thank him for what he did for my country." This was a side of Stathis I had not seen before and it made me like him even more.

The view from atop the hill was magnificent. It provided a three-hundred-and-sixty-degree panorama of Athens and the surrounding countryside. Stathis proudly showed me the Plaka and the Agora and other famous sights. He was obviously proud of his city as we gazed at the beauty spread before us. Of course, his attention soon came back to me, and we were off to the Hotel Arethusa again for some afternoon shenanigans. By now, I was looking forward to being with him, to once again be intimately connected to a man who said he loved me. Life was good again.

We spent two weeks together. He showed me all the sights of Athens and I had a wonderful time.

The day before I was to leave for Canada, he didn't show up at the usual time. After a while, I called him.

"Stathis, where are you?" I said.

"I am in my engine," he answered gruffly.

"But tomorrow is my last day in Greece. I won't see you again until Christmas."

"I will come tomorrow to say goodbye," he said.

I spent a restless night wondering if I had imagined the whole time we had been together. I had felt so close to him, and now he made me doubt his declarations of love.

He showed up just as I was getting ready to leave the hotel in a taxi.

"I will drive you to the airport," he said.

On the way, he talked about the repairs he had to make to his car. Parts are expensive in Greece and he complained about having to use his winnings from the casino to keep the old Chevy going.

"Maybe I can't come to see you in Canada. I can't afford the airplane ticket," he said. He looked sad as he took my hand and kissed it. I felt sorry for him.

"I can help you, Stathis. Tell me how much money you need and I will send it to you."

"Thank you, Mary." He seemed to brighten up as I walked away to board the plane.

"I will see you soon. You will show me a Canada Christmas, *ne*? There will be snow?"

"Yiassou," I said. I was sure I was falling in love again and it filled me with hope and a warm glow.

When I got home Barbara could hardly wait to tell me she had had another interesting call. It was from a Mrs. Marinakis who had found this strange number on her husband's cell phone.

"Hello, Varvara?" she said.

"Yes," said my sister.

"Stathis will not be coming to visit you in Canada. I am calling to let you know. He does not love you."

"But, Mrs. Marinakis, it's my sister who knows your husband, not me. She will be very surprised. He said he was divorced."

"I know, I know," she said wearily. "It's not her fault. I know my Stathis. You tell her for me. I am sorry."

It didn't surprise me. I was learning a lot about men now that I was on my own for the first time since I married at nineteen. No matter how nice they seemed, men tell lies to get what they want. I should have listened to the wizened little old Greek lady I met on the way home on Olympic Airways.

A basket of food lay at her feet. When the beverage carts came out she waved the stewardess away and took a large loaf of bread from her basket.

"No eat that," she said, shoving the bread in my face. "Eat this."

I broke off a hunk and started to chew. "Are you coming to Canada on a holiday?" I asked.

"No, I live in Montreal. I have a house in Athens. I just go home to clean the steps. No one cleans the steps but me." She rubbed her back with both hands and grimaced.

"Why you go to Greece?" she said.

I thought maybe I could make her smile. "To find a rich husband like Aristotle Onassis," I said.

"You stay home, marry nice Canada man," she said emphatically, waving her breadstick under my nose. "Greek men are shit."

Chapter 13 - The Scout

One evening in early November, I looked out the window of my cottage on Lake Erie to catch a glimpse of the sunset lighting up the smokestacks of Hydro One at Nanticoke.

That's when I saw them. A great, gray crowd of Canada geese standing up to their shins in water on the rocky shingle we call the beach. There must have been a hundred of them, all different sizes, youngsters and older birds, preening and dipping their beaks in and out of the shallow water, stretching their necks and flapping their wings. I hadn't heard them arrive, but as I watched I became aware of an excited ripple passing through their ranks. Something was afoot. Great swaths of yellow and orange lit up the clouds and kept darkness from closing in as the elders among the feathered throng stood up tall and beat the air, first one and then another until the great horde was in motion. Without thinking, I turned to tell Paul to come and witness this amazing invasion, then remembered he was no longer there. It had been three years since his death, but still my first instinct was to share the sight with him. When would I ever remember that I was now alone?

I turned back to the window just in time to see four stalwart birds rise into the air as though in response to some unheard command. They skimmed low over the surface of the water and then rose high into the sky peeling off in four different directions, north, south, east and west, until gradually each one disappeared from view among the darkening clouds.

The ones that were left were quieter now and rested on the waves, waiting patiently, perhaps settling down for the night, I thought. But after about an hour, one of the scouts returned and skidded in for a landing on the narrow strip of water that opened magically in the midst of his comrades. He was greeted by a flutter of excitement that set the other geese chattering and flapping their wings, beating the water into foamy waves. Another scout splashed down, and another, honking the news about what they had seen. All at once, after about half an hour, the group rose up into the air, a silent gray squadron gradually arranging themselves into their familiar V shape as they headed southwest out toward Long Point Bay on the first leg of their long journey south.

But where was scout number four? He hadn't returned with the others. The flock was fast disappearing out toward the horizon where the navy-blue sky now blended seamlessly into the black water. I began to worry. How would he know where to find them when he returned? I waited anxiously by the window. It was almost dark when he reappeared at last, coming in for a smooth landing on the empty surface of the lake. He looked around, walked up and down, searching it seemed, for some sign of his missing companions, some clue to let him know which way they had gone. My heart went out to him as he waited. Go. Go that way, I thought. I wanted to walk down to the water's edge and point it out for him, but I knew he wouldn't understand.

We waited a long time. Me, anxiously at my window and him, swimming in lonely circles on the empty water. At last he took off. Thank goodness, I thought. He might still catch up to them. The moon gave me a brief glimpse of him as he rose into the dark sky, and my heart sank. He was going the wrong way, back east the way he had come. I watched in helpless silence. He would be alone forever now, like me. My heart ached for him and I felt tears spilling down my cheeks.

And then at the last moment, just before he disappeared from view, something made him change his mind and I saw him veer to starboard, slowly, slowly, bringing his flight path back in line with the ones that had left him behind. At my last sight of him he had kicked up his speed a notch and was beating strongly into the dark sky, alone, heading southwest, following the path of the moon on the water to find his own kind. I like to think he had heard my heart calling out to him.

Chapter 14 - Old Men Need Not Apply

On the day he died, my husband put down his beer and said to his friend standing nearby, "When is *that woman* ever going to be finished making me renovate things?" These were his last words. I suppose I should have been glad that at least he died thinking of me. But I have felt ever since that I was somehow responsible for his early and sudden departure from this earth.

After a long while of missing him terribly, I began to long for the company of a man my own age. I had been alone long enough for all the clichés about widows to show up in my life. My married girl friends, husbands in tow, went their merry ways without me. Married women don't like odd numbers and have an inherent mistrust of widows. I was left to my wonderful, single women friends and my own devices. I do not do lonely very well and I wanted a man of my own. After all, I was only sixty-two.

Fortunately, a former neighbour lost his wife, and we began a friendship. Soon, I found myself hoping it would blossom into something wonderful. He was tall, good-looking, funny and quite well-off. We had fun together.

Unfortunately, he cut the lawn one hot summer day and dropped dead. I was very sad.

Moments on a Staircase

A few months later, an old girlfriend of mine died and her husband was left alone. He had been the best man at my wedding years ago and we had kept in touch all that time. It seemed quite natural for us to drift together and since I had known him for so long, it was easy. He was tall and good-looking and funny and a very sweet man.

He went to the hospital one day to have some fluid drained from his legs.

"I'll be coming home on the week-end," he said. "We'll go out for dinner Saturday night."

Sadly, he died in the hospital and I never saw him again.

I developed a phobia about older men. It seemed to me that every time I got close to one, they expired. I felt like a black widow who sucks the juice out of her mate and leaves him a dry husk to blow away in the wind. I bought a t-shirt that said, *"We could mate, but then I'd have to kill you."* I frightened all my relatives when I wore it to the family picnic. My sons started to watch me with worried expressions on their faces.

I soon realized I was single-handedly decimating the small population of available men in their seventies, given the tendency of females to outlive their male counterparts. For the sake of this fragile demographic, I decided to focus my attention on younger men. They were a healthy and willing bunch and I didn't have to worry about killing them. They seemed to appear like magic at the door of my new condo: the furniture delivery guy, the guy who hooked up my dishwasher, the painter, the drapery man who sold blinds. The tinker, the tailor, the soldier, the sailor; all hale and hearty and quite happy to spend some time with a lonely old widow. If you give them enough beer, or wine and turn down the lights, they don't seem to notice the wrinkles or the gray hair or the flabby arms.

Moments on a Staircase

But I hadn't taken into account the fact that I was not getting any younger. After two hip replacements and shoulder surgery when one of my paramours bounced me right off the bed onto the floor I decided young men were too much for me. Besides, they were not what I wanted. I wanted what I had had for forty-three years; a man I could love, a man who loved me too, a man of my own.

I found an internet dating site for "mature adults". It was called *Auld Lang Syne*. I joined up eagerly and waited with anticipation for my first date. True to their word, they sent me pictures every day of the available men in my area.

They were usually dark, shadowy, unsmiling selfies of old guys claiming to be sixty-four when they looked like they were on their last legs. They gave themselves some colourful monikers, like LUV2KISS, and UMEWOW. The most graphic one was KONGFUCK which conjured up a scary scenario that made me wince. But I had paid for three months worth, so I decided to stop being so judgemental and picked out three of the best of them. I sent each of them a heart icon and waited to see what would happen.

I got a date immediately with SWEETYPIE, an interesting looking man who was pictured in a suit and tie sitting at a desk. He looked like a businessman and had a pleasant smile and a bit of hair. We made a date to meet for a coffee at the restaurant across the street from my condo. His name was Rolfe. He was already seated at a booth when I walked in, but we recognized each other right away, even though he looked a bit older than his profile proclaimed. We ended up talking for quite a while, making pleasant conversation. I began to think maybe he was a possibility. He seemed to like me and laughed at my jokes and best of all, he paid for the coffee.

When we stood up to leave, he was only about five feet tall. I towered over him as he helped me on with my jacket. Before I had a chance to get used to the idea of the difference in our heights, it became irrelevant.

"I notice you have big boobs," he whispered seductively in my ear as his hands brushed against my chest. "Let's get together again soon."

"I'm sorry," I said, "I have a fatal disease."

When I got home I thought of all the things I should have said. Like, "I notice you have a small dick." But I didn't. He called several times but I didn't answer, and then he gave up.

I gave up too, for a while. Then the loneliness settled in again and I realized that I had two months left on my contract, so I crept back to my dating site.

This time I vowed to be more diligent in my choices, to look more carefully at the candidates presented to me, to study their profiles carefully, to read between the lines. No more naïve little innocent. Back on the website, the *Your Selections* button produced the same tired, old photos of the same tired, old men, with one exception, LOVE2MEET. He had submitted several pictures of himself; on holiday in Greece, with children in a lovely-looking home, playing with a small dog in his beautifully landscaped back yard, in a captain's hat on the deck of a sailboat. He looked tall as he leaned over the wheel of the boat, and he was tanned and handsome and healthy looking. My heart leaped. Maybe, just maybe, he would be my Mr. Right.

He answered my gift of a heart immediately with an invitation to lunch. I again suggested the restaurant across the street from my condo, and we arranged to meet the next day. I was nervous and excited as I got ready to go out. New hairdo, new top, new perfume. When I looked in the mirror, I laughed at myself and thought, "This poor guy doesn't stand a chance." It turned out even better than I had hoped. He was tall and good-looking, well-spoken, interesting and lots of fun. We spent two hours talking and laughing together and made the beginning of a great connection with each other. When it came time to leave, we were both reluctant to go. As he held the door for me, he put his hand on my arm and I felt an electric thrill go through me. This could be it. How lucky could I get?

"Thanks for the lunch," I said. "It was fun. If you want to call me again, please do." I never heard from him again. I like to think he was hit by a train on his way home.

But, I am not easily discouraged. When my hormones sputtered into action again a few weeks later, I went back to *Auld Lang Syne*. This time I took a fancy to a nice-looking man who called himself MAGICMORTY. I checked his profile thoroughly looking for any signs of deviant behaviour. When I read that the person he admired most was Morgan Freeman, I relaxed. Could anyone who listed 'God' as his favourite be less than stellar? Not only that, he played bridge and golf and loved to travel. He said he owned several time-shares around the world; South Carolina, Florida, Scotland, Portugal and Belize. He also volunteered for several local charities and put on magic shows at retirement homes in the city. I thought I had hit the motherlode. When we met for a drink at a little bistro, things got even better. He was fascinating to talk to and he seemed to enjoy listening to my stories. We laughed and sipped our wine and I could feel myself warming to him. He even made a date to take me for dinner the following night to a very nice restaurant in town. This one is it, I thought. My search for true love is over at last. He walked me to my car and when I turned to say goodbye he put his arms around me and pulled me in for a kiss. I closed my eyes and offered my lips to his.

Moments on a Staircase

He had no lips. At least that's how it seemed. I moved mine around and couldn't find his at all. When I opened my eyes, all I saw was the inside of his mouth gaping at me; teeth, tongue and all, right back to his uvula swaying in the breeze. He had opened his mouth so wide I could have performed a tonsillectomy with my teeth. I had the fleeting fear he was going to Hoover me up and swallow me whole. I recoiled in horror. We parted, but later that night I received an e-mail from him cancelling our date for dinner.

"I'm afraid your libido doesn't match mine," he said, "and that's a deal-breaker for me. I hope you find a man who doesn't mind your lack of interest in sex. Good luck."

I fired back a nasty note of my own, "I hope you find some woman who likes to make out in the parking lot of a restaurant in broad daylight with a man she doesn't know. She shouldn't be too hard to find. I think they're called hookers."

And abracadabra, just like that, MAGICMORTY vanished into cyberspace and I was alone again.

A friend took me to the SPCA and I found a scruffy old alley cat that was ready for euthanasia. I took him home and was sure we would become fast friends. After all, were two of a kind. We were both in the checkout line and nobody wanted us. I call him Louie. I think this could be the start of a beautiful friendship ... if he would just come out from behind the sofa

Moments on a Staircase

Chapter 15 - My Porkchop

Every woman ought to have a porkchop of her own. I am one of the lucky ones. His name is Jose Manuel Barbosa DaCosta. He sauntered through my garden gate one hot, summer day and knocked me off my rocker.

I was sitting on the patio of my new condo that day, reading *The Theban Plays of Sophocles*. That's just how exciting my life had become since my husband dropped dead suddenly a few years before. My efforts to replace him had been futile. In a desperate bid to find some reason to keep on living, I imagined that I would take up writing as a hobby. In university, I had been fascinated with the story of Oedipus and Jocasta, and I remember feeling that she had really gotten a bum rap, both in the play and life itself. The focus is always on Oedipus, of course, and I had some kind of off-the-wall notion that I would re-write the story from Jocasta's point of view. Such hubris would have shocked even the most daring of Greeks.

So engrossed was I in their tragic story, I didn't notice the stranger standing on the other side of my trellis gate. He coughed softly and I looked up to see a short, swarthy-looking man wearing the yellow shirt of the Corelli Landscape Company. Obviously, he was one of an army of anonymous workers who swarmed over the condo complex that July planting endless rolls of sod on the bare earth. I thought he looked quite handsome in a rugged, earthy way.

Thick dark hair grew low on his forehead and black stubble covered a strong, square chin. His lips were nicely shaped, the lower one full and sensuous. Patches of sweat outlined a strong muscular chest beneath the thin material of his shirt. Swipes of reddish dirt marked his face where he had obviously tried to wipe the stinging wetness away from his eyes. I could see that his shorts were actually old jeans, badly worn and cut off roughly, the hem clumsily sewn by hand with black thread. The big childish stitches stood out against the faded blue that encircled his heavy thighs. A kind of girdle made of dark cloth was strapped to his waist, obviously meant to hold his back in place for the heavy lifting he did. I wondered how long he had been there watching. He peered up at me from under the brim of his cap.

"Hi," he said, with a slight smile. His hand remained on the gate, apparently waiting for an invitation to enter. "Do you have a glass of water for me?" he asked politely.

"Come on in. I'll go and get you one. You can sit down if you like." He opened the gate and took a cautious step into the garden. His heavy work boots were covered with dust and quite large for his height. He was stocky, powerfully built; close to the ground that he tilled for a living. As he moved to the chair opposite me, I realized I was quite a bit taller than him. It was as though he was meant to be taller, but his legs didn't match the rest of his body. They had failed somehow to fulfill their intended proportions.

He took off his hat, then dusted the back of his shorts with his hands, lowering himself gingerly into the aluminum lawn chair, looking out of place and uncomfortable.

Moments on a Staircase

"Would you rather have a beer?" I asked.

His smile widened. "Yes please, that would be nice."

When I came back he reached for it with a look of gratitude.

"*Tank* you," he said.

"You're welcome." I replied.

He settled back in the chair, his eyes never leaving my face. I felt that he was looking at me the way a construction worker on the street might size up a woman passing by. What was the matter with him? I was sixty-four years old, for God's sake. No one had looked at me like that in years. Heat rose from my chest up into my cheeks. I looked down at my feet, unable to think of anything to say to him.

He tipped the bottle up to his lips and tilted his head back to drink. Heat and sweat had made several dirty rings around his neck. When it was empty, he set the bottle down carefully on the table, then leaned forward, clasping his two large hands together as he rested his forearms on his knees. His gold-flecked eyes seemed to be probing into me.

"What are you reading?" he asked.

I struggled to think of a way to describe *The Oedipus Plays of Sophocles* to this seemingly uneducated labourer speaking heavily accented English. The teacher in me made me decide to give it a try.

"It's a story about a young man who kills his father and marries his mother and has children with her." I watched his face, not really sure he even understood what I had said. He looked towards the sky, frowning and muttered something in his native tongue. To me, it sounded like he was calling on God to protect him from these perverse words coming out of my mouth.

"I guess you don't want me to tell you the rest of it." I made no effort to keep the sarcasm out of my voice.

He fixed me with that penetrating stare again. "I want to hear. Tell me."

I took a deep breath and continued.

"The man's name was Oedipus and before he was born, his parents, who were the King and Queen of Thebes, went to a sacred place in Greece called Delphi. There was an oracle there, a kind of priest who told them they would have a son who would grow up to kill his father. So they went home and when their first child was a baby boy they gave him to a shepherd to take out into the hills and leave for the wolves to eat so he couldn't grow up and kill his father." I watched the man as he listened raptly to the story.

"They should have stayed away from that place," he said. "That priest was stupid."

"You're right." I smiled at the simplicity of his reply. "But they believed him, so they gave away their son to be killed."

"He should never have given away his son." His tone was contemptuous. "What kind of a man would do this? I would never give my son away. That's it."

A shrug of his shoulders signalled his disdain and an apparent end to his interest in the story. He held the empty bottle out to me.

"I could drink another beer."

I began to feel uneasy. I was running out of things to say to him and I didn't want him to get into trouble.

"Aren't you supposed to be working?"

"Yes, but I am the boss," he asserted proudly. "I am the foreman of this crew. They do what I say. Me, Joe. This guy here." He stabbed his thumbs into his chest as he spoke. Then a slight smile turned up the corners of his mouth, giving him a sly, knowing expression. "And Gino Corelli has gone home for the day. It is too hot for him." His burst of laughter was engaging, lighting up his face, making him look even younger.

My interest was aroused by this flash of humour from my strange guest. I felt myself warming to him.

"Are you Italian, Joe?"

Quickly, the laughter stopped and his lip curled into a sneer. "No, I am Portuguese." He watched my face closely as if to see how I would react to this news. I tried to remain impassive but I sensed I had insulted him in some way. They all looked the same to me; dark, and somehow dangerous. I tried to make amends.

"I'll get you that beer now." I hoped he would see that I was open-minded about his heritage, that it made no difference to me. I had always liked to think of myself as liberal-minded. When I returned with the beer, he tilted the bottle up against his lower lip and drank noisily until it was empty.

"That was good, *tank* you." He set the bottle down, but made no move to leave. I started to wonder if I would have trouble getting rid of him. The analogy of the camel's nose in the Bedouin's tent crossed my mind. I decided to tell him I was out of beer if he asked for another.

But something about him fascinated me. I forgot my reservations for the moment and continued the conversation. After all, I had nothing else to do and perhaps he might even give me some primitive insight into the tragic story I was trying to understand. He could certainly cut through the crap and get to the meat of it.

"Do you want to hear some more of the story, Joe?" I found it hard to say his name, it didn't suit his exotic looks.

"Why not?" He settled back in his chair, fixing his eyes politely on my face.

I plunged in once again.

"Remember, they gave their son to a shepherd. But he had a kind heart and he couldn't leave the baby boy out on the rocks to die, so he gave him to the king and queen of a nearby city, Corinth. They had no children, so they were happy to have the baby. They named him Oedipus. One day, when he was a grown man, Oedipus was driving his chariot along the road and he came to a crossroad." I made an X shape with my hands in case he didn't understand, but Joe nodded his head, waving off this gesture and I continued. "He met an older man in a chariot coming from the other direction. He was in the young man's way, but he wouldn't move over to let him get past. So, they fought and the young man killed the older man, who just happened to be--"

"His father," Joe interrupted. He was on the edge of his seat now. "Why didn't the old guy go around him? Was there room to go around?"

Recalling my travels, I remember seeing the fabled place where Oedipus killed his father and there had indeed been room for the two chariots to pass each other. This strange visitor of mine had stripped the famous Greek tragedy down to a few rudimentary facts. It could all have been avoided with a little common sense from these two hot-heads, father and son.

"Yes, there was lots of room. Too bad you weren't there to tell them what to do, but since you weren't, do you want me to tell you what happened next?"

He nodded, suddenly solemn, looking like a chastened schoolboy as he waited in silence for me to continue. He peered quizzically up at me when I took up the story again.

"Oedipus went to the city called Thebes where the older man he had just killed came from. Outside the gate of the city was a monster called the Sphinx, who had been terrorizing the people. To get into the city, the young man had to answer a riddle that the Sphinx asked. Do you understand this word, riddle?"

"Oh yes, like that guy in Batman."

I smiled and nodded. "If he gives the wrong answer, the creature will kill him, but if he answers the riddle correctly, he will become the new king. Do you want to hear the riddle?"

"Go ahead. Riddle me." Joe challenged me with a cocky look as he leaned back in his chair. Once again, I took a breath and forged ahead, knowing he was in beyond his depth.

"Here it is then. 'What walks on four legs in the morning, two legs in the afternoon and three legs at night?'"

He tipped his head to one side and frowned. "Four legs...two legs...three legs," he mumbled under his breath.

And then, suddenly self-assured, he looked up and smiled.

"A man. When he was a baby, four legs. A man, two legs and then..." Joe jumped out of his chair and became an old man walking with a cane, "three legs, you see? That's it."

I tried to keep the look of amazement from my face. He was right!

"Good for you." I wondered if he had heard the riddle before, but his reaction appeared to be spontaneous and immediate. Once again, I suppressed a smile.

"Now he can be king." There was genuine delight in Joe's voice.

"Yes, now he can be king. And not only that, he gets to marry the widow of the king. Do you understand 'widow'? Her husband is dead, so she is now a widow."

He nodded. "*Viúva*, that's how we say it in my country."

"Vay-oo-vuh". I pursed my lips the way he did and tried it several times as he nodded his approval.

"I am a *viúva*," I told him. The look in his eyes softened. A slight shrug of his shoulders implied some sympathy, but he didn't speak. Time seemed to stretch out long and silent in the hot summer air as we stared at each other. I felt like I was drifting away into some other time and space, captivated by his eyes. At last I roused myself to speak, breaking the spell. "The *viúva* belongs to the young man now, so she will be his wife. Remember, she is his mother, the one who gave him away...but...he doesn't know that and neither does she. So, he marries her, and they have four children, two daughters and two sons. They are his children, but also his brothers and sisters. And they are her children and her grandchildren too. What a mess, eh?" I wondered if he had been able to follow this complicated plot.

"Holy shit. It's all fucked up!" Joe looked down at the patio for a moment, then back directly into my eyes. "But he didn't know?"

"No, he didn't know. Oedipus was happy and he loved his wife. Her name was Jocasta." I took a sip of my drink and watched the frown on Joe's face deepen as he digested this information.

Suddenly he burst out, "It wasn't his fault. He didn't know. That's it." Joe raised his hands and turned his face heavenward with a fatalistic shrug of resignation to those inexplicable gods who control the fates of men.

"But wait, it isn't over yet." I felt compelled to tell him the rest of the disastrous story, to finish what I had started. "The shepherd comes back and tells Oedipus and Jocasta the truth and Jocasta hangs herself. When Oedipus sees her hanging there he reaches into her apron pocket and takes out her scissors and shoves the points into his eyes and blinds himself. Then he is thrown out of Thebes by the people and he spends the rest of his life wandering around with his daughters, begging from town to town."

Joe's expression this time was one of genuine disgust.

"This is not the kind of story you should be reading. This is too much. Why do you read such stuff?"

I felt I had lost his respect and scrambled to explain. "I am writing a book about the mother, Jocasta. Nobody thinks about her side of the story. I want to find out why she hung herself. Was it because she was so ashamed of what they had done, or was it because she really loved Oedipus and knew she could never be with him again? Can a woman love a man young enough to be her son and could he really fall in love with her?"

This last question hovered between us in the stifling heat. We stared at each other for several seconds and then slowly his expression changed. The golden sparks in the gasoline-coloured pools of his eyes caught fire in the hot sun. I looked away, but not before I felt he had detected something lurking inside me, some dark and dreadful secret I had hidden, even from myself. Flustered, I tried to think of something to say. My mouth went dry.

"Do you have children, Joe?" The question broke the tension and seemed to restore the distance between us.

"Yes, I have a son. His name is Brian. He is *tree* years old. I am old to be his father. I was tirty when he was born. Now I am tirty-tree." He paused and rolled his eyes toward the heavens. "Just like the one up there." One of his large hands moved to cover his heart. "He was tirty-tree when they killed him, you know."

I was surprised at this sudden piety.

"Are you Catholic?"

"Yes." He watched my face intently, but once again I managed to remain impassive. It seemed wise to avoid the religious angle. So far, he seemed to have a few prejudices. Italians, Jews. I wondered what he might think if he knew I was Irish. As if he could read my thoughts, he asked about my name.

"I have heard people call you Mary." He was watching me with one eye again.

"I'm really Mary Ellen, but everyone calls me Mary. My father was Irish. He named me Mary. You can call me Mary, if you like."

"Like Mary Magdalene, neh?" He nodded his head, prompting me to remember. "In the Bible, you know, she was the one who washed Jesus' feet with her tears and dried them with her hair. She was a prostitute but Jesus didn't mind."

Once more I decided to steer the conversation away from religion.

"Do you have any other children, Joe?"

"No, just my son. He is very smart." He blew into his fingers and they flew apart in a gesture obviously meant to illustrate the child's mental superiority. During my years as a teacher, I had often seen this look on the faces of parents. Joe was obviously proud of his son.

"He loves me too. Whenever he sees me he runs up to me and says, 'Daddy, daddy, what did you bringed me?' and he reaches into my pocket to see what is in there for him. Sometimes I take him pretty stones that I find and he puts them in a jar. Maybe I will take one of these stones you have here for him." He indicated the decorative marble chips laid artistically around the edge of my garden to keep the weeds at bay.

I shrugged my indifference. I was beginning to feel like Barbara Walters, probing the circumstances of this stranger's life, amusing myself with his unusual sounding speech and the peculiar gestures of his culture. But I had to admit, something about him fascinated me. I liked the way he talked, the resonant timbre of his voice, the blatant masculinity of the man. And he seemed to be intelligent and obviously very fond of his son. I had to admit I didn't want the conversation to end.

"And your wife, Joe, what does she do?"

"We are divorced. I live with my mother, in her house." An angry look clouded his features. It was disturbing since it followed so closely the loving expression that had accompanied his words about his son.

Unable to stop myself I pressed on, "Does he live with you?"

"I see him on Thursdays and Sundays." He closed one eye as he tilted his head to observe the effect of his words. Why did he do this? Was it some kind of Portuguese signal, perhaps a warning to discontinue this line of conversation?

Before I could react, he turned the discussion toward more pleasant things.

"Do you like to eat sausages?" He leaned forward, watching my face.

"Actually," I admitted, "sausages are not my favourite food."

His demeanor changed radically, from sinister to childlike. He sprang up enthusiastically from his chair.

"But my mother makes the best sausages in the world," he said. Then magnanimously, "I will bring you some. Are you busy tomorrow night?"

I was having trouble keeping up with him. What was he saying? How could I keep him from coming back and hanging around? Once you let these people in you can never get rid of them...like the Jehovah's Witnesses who linger persistently at my door on Sunday mornings.

But all I could manage to say was, "No, I am never busy."

He smiled, looking pleased with himself. "Good. I will pass by about seven o'clock. I will cook the sausages for you. You will like them, you will see. That's it."

He picked up his hat, put it on backwards and ambled to the gate, bending over on his way to pick up a shiny white stone from the edge of the flower bed. The large muscles of his calves bulged as he bent to his task. Then he straightened up and passed beneath the trellis, his steps rolling and insolent. He didn't notice the love-lies-bleeding that had been crushed beneath one of his heavy boots, leaving a scarlet stain on the concrete of the patio. Turning back, he smiled at me again and closed the trellis gate.

"Tanks for the beers and for this." He held up the small bit of marble. "I will see you tomorrow night around seven, seven-tirty." And he was gone.

Moments on a Staircase

The garden seemed suddenly empty and colorless without him, somehow depleted of its vitality. I picked up my glass, took a big swallow and sighed. Oh, God. What had I done now? I didn't know this guy from a hole in the ground. And I hated sausages. But I felt something begin to stir inside my hollow place. A little sliver of warmth had somehow been rekindled there.   The next morning I awoke in a tangle of bedclothes and pillows. The ceiling fan was still turning quietly, but the air seemed cooler even without its help. Thank goodness because I don't function well in the heat. And the thought of what might lie ahead that evening made me grateful that I wouldn't have to put up with the uncomfortable weather as well as the awkward situation I had managed to get myself into. What if he came, that guy, Joe? What would I do with him?

I spooned coffee into the coffee maker and turned it on. The newspaper lay waiting on my front porch and as I picked it up I waved to the nameless gray-haired woman across the street who was watering her new grass. I could never remember her name although she had introduced herself when she moved in. Katharine, Karen, something like that. I wondered what the neighbours would think if my new friend showed up. They'd seen him around the condo property working with his landscaping crew. They'd recognize him. Oh shit!

Then my common sense took over. He wouldn't come. He was just bragging about his mother's cooking to impress me. Why on earth would he want to spend time with an old lady like me? He had probably forgotten all about it by now. I decided to dismiss my fears that he'd show up, and to ignore the slight disappointment I felt once I had convinced myself he wouldn't come. It would make a good story to tell at bridge next week. A little smile pulled up the corners of my mouth as I imagined what the girls would say.

Moments on a Staircase

You did what? You told him the story of Oedipus *and* Jocasta? *And then you let him cook sausages for you? You're crazy*!

After I read the paper and downed three cups of coffee, I turned on my computer and tried to write. But it was hard to concentrate. My thoughts kept returning to the man, Joe. I opened the blinds in the kitchen and looked up and down the street. There was no sign of him. No noisy machinery, no cloud of dust to betray the whereabouts of the landscaping crew. His work must have taken him to some other area of the property today. By noon I had given up on my writing. After lunch I changed into my old jeans and went to the basement to empty some of the boxes that still stood two or three deep against the edges of the cement block walls. A lifetime's accumulation of treasures and junk. They had been lined up there since I moved in a few months ago. Unpacking them seemed like a never-ending task, like cleaning the Augean Stables, and the recollections they brought back always made me sad. By three o'clock I had unpacked only one box was made miserable by the memories found inside: my wedding album, Paul's bronze lifesaving medal, somebody's little white baby shoes. I was ready for a nap. But not before taking a quick peek out of the window again to see if I could see the landscapers working nearby. Nothing.

By six o'clock I was sure he wouldn't come. But at six-thirty I found myself in the bathroom looking in the mirror. I put on some lipstick and fluffed up my hair with my fingers. Just in case. The face that smiled back at me was vibrant and somehow expectant. I turned sideways and looked critically at the t-shirt I had on. It showed too much padding around my middle. Damn the bastard who invented spandex! I put on a loose shirt from the closet, turning this way and that in front of the mirror, pulling in my stomach, smiling sideways and tossing my head coquettishly. Then I laughed out loud, but it was a bitter sound.

What the hell was I doing? He was just a kid. And he wasn't coming. At least I hoped he wasn't.

But at precisely seven o'clock I heard a sharp rap at the front door. I could see his outline through the coloured glass sidelight, the short burly shape with the dark hair. My heart started to race. Why the hell had I said he could come? I didn't really know anything about him. He could be planning to rob and murder me. I must have been out of my mind. I could pretend to be out. Maybe he hadn't seen the light on in the kitchen. He knocked again, this time with more force. I could imagine that large strong hand balled up into a fist, making contact with the steel door, commanding it to be opened. His shadow in the window grew larger as he tried to peer through its etched surface into the hallway where I stood, backed up in a corner as far as I could go, cringing there, hardly breathing.

Then slowly I pushed myself away from the safety of the wall and walked to the door. This is stupid. If he kills me, so what? He would be doing me a favour. For a moment I imagined those strong fingers closing around my throat, ending the pain I had felt since Paul died.

I reached out to unlock the door and slowly opened it, peering around the edge directly into his eyes. The gaze he sent back at me was steady but not homicidal. He looked amused. Half-hidden behind the door I hesitated, still not sure of what I should say to him.

"It's me, Joe, remember?" he said, thrusting a long thin package wrapped in a plastic bag towards me. "Here's the sausage I told you about, neh?" A smile lit up his face and melted away my fear as I opened the door fully to let him in.

He was wearing a clean white t-shirt that emphasized the tanned skin of his face and neck. His hair was shiny and slicked back from his low forehead. On his feet were white socks and a pair of flip-flops, the bare legs above large and muscular and liberally dusted with dark hair. His face was clean-shaven, and the high cheekbones were polished from their recent scrubbing. He looked quite handsome except for the ridiculous footwear. I stepped back a bit to let him pass and smelled a heavy dose of cologne, something cheap and almost feminine which didn't suit the maleness that exuded from his very pores. He seemed more like a lady- killer than a murderer.

"Come on in," I said. With a sweeping gesture I waved him into the kitchen indicating a chair at the table, but instead he walked straight to the counter near the stove turning abruptly to ask,

"Do you have a pot?"

Surprised, I reached around him to open the cupboard near his knees. He looked inside but made no move to take out one of the shiny stainless pots of various sizes stacked neatly on the shelves.

"What kind of a pot?" I asked, pointing to the obviously well-stocked cupboard. Seeing his reluctance to reach in and get one, I pulled out a medium-sized pot with a lid and offered it to him. "Like this?"

"No. Not like that. Don't you have a pot to put on the top of the stove, a flat one with a handle?" He was obviously trying to be patient with me.

"Oh, do you mean a frying pan?" I opened the bottom drawer of the stove selecting a pan which I set up on top.

"Yes, this is good". He seemed pleased that \I was becoming more co-operative. "Now I will take that sausage that I gave you." He extended his hand and I placed the package he had given me into his palm. He faced the sink and turned on the tap. I watched in surprise as he rinsed the pan under the running water for several seconds. He was washing the fucking pan!

"Do you have a cloth to dry it?" he asked.

Once again, I had to reach around him to the cabinet where my kitchen towels hung. My body rubbed against his side as he made no effort to get out of the way. I pulled back, embarrassed, as I felt the hardness and the heat of him burning into me.

Why didn't he move? And why was I feeling this current of electricity passing through my insides? There was no denying the hypnotic male aura that I felt whenever I got too close.

"Here you go." I said. I handed him a dish towel and watched him dry the pan with great care, then set it on my new stainless-steel stove. He looked at the smooth ceramic top with a puzzled frown.

"Where are the hot places for cooking?"

I tried not to laugh. Obviously, he had never seen the latest trend in flat top stoves. I drew little circles in the air above the outlines of the burners and was about to show him how to turn them on, when he interrupted with an imperious wave of his hand.

"Make it hot, please." With an exaggerated flourish I obeyed his commands like some kind of menial kitchen help bowing to the demands of the master. Whom did this arrogant little character think he was, taking over my kitchen and giving orders like some great Cordon Bleu chef?

"Do you have any oil?" he said.

I pointed dramatically with both hands to the olive oil in its large, distinctive bottle sitting in plain view on the counter. Then I watched in amazement as he poured half of it into the pan. It would take me six months to use that much oil. I began to wonder if he knew what he was doing, but I didn't have time to protest. He was extracting an ugly reddish-brown object from the plastic bag. With a look of tenderness on his face, he held it up for me to admire.

"This," he intoned reverently, "is Momma's sausage." Then, in a flash, he held it upright in one hand and moved it to the front of his shorts, waving it up and down and looking at me with the naughty expression of an impudent boy. His laughter was loud and spontaneous as he gestured with his sausage, looking slyly at me, encouraging me to laugh with him. When I failed to join in, he frowned, perhaps thinking I hadn't understood his little stunt. I felt distaste for his childish humour but at the same time the whole ludicrous situation made it hard to keep from laughing out loud. What was he doing in my kitchen waving a sausage around, pretending it was his dick? And why in God's name was I letting him? I wondered just how much more ridiculous things would get before he was through.

As the oil in the pan began to sizzle, Joe reverted once more to his serious chef persona. Carefully, as though he were putting a baby down for a nap, he slid the precious sausage into the pan where it lay drowning and sputtering in the hot oil. With a look of satisfaction he leaned over to inhale the pungent aroma, eyes closed.

"Mmmm, no one makes sausages like my mother."

I didn't mind the spicy smell beginning to fill the kitchen.

"Can you get me that *another* pot now? I need it for the rice," he said.

He rinsed this one too and dried it carefully before filling it with water. I tried to anticipate his needs, turning the burner on for him once more. He didn't seem to get the hang of my stove. I began to wonder if maybe I had been wrong about him being smart.

"Do you have some rice?" He looked around but didn't touch the doors to the cupboards. I now began to get the picture. This was my job.

"Rice? What kind of rice?" I said. It had been ages since I had cooked rice and when I did, I usually made a bad job of it, turning it into a sticky glob of starch despite my best intentions. Joe was looking at me now with ill-disguised pity.

"Ordinary rice like you cook every day. It's white, like little seeds." He spoke slowly and put two of his big fingers together to try to help me envision the size of the grains.

"I know what rice looks like," I said as I tossed my head at him, chin up.

"I have all kinds of rice." I wasn't sure this was true, but this little Portuguese pipsqueak was really starting to get on my nerves.

As if he sensed my feelings, Joe's voice took on a more conciliatory tone.

"Please, I need the rice now. The water is jumping." He indicated the boiling water with one hand. "And some vinegar too... if you have some." He sounded doubtful.

I searched through the cans and boxes in my pantry and came up with the required items. In silence I placed them on the counter in front of him and watched, fascinated, as he shook the grains of rice from the bag into the pot without measuring them. Reaching around his shoulder carefully so I wouldn't touch him, I selected a wooden spoon from the jar of utensils beside the stove and began to stir the rice as it lay in a mound beneath the bubbling water. Suddenly, my wrist was encircled tightly by one of his big hands.

"No . . .no . . .don't touch it. Never stir the rice. My mother told me when I was little, just leave it alone . . . don't even look at it."

He pulled the spoon from my hands and waved me to a chair at the table, my cheeks stained pink with the sting of his rebuke, a stranger in my own kitchen. Clearly this was his domain now. Apparently, I was there simply to do what he said, too inept even to stir a pot on the stove. What a nervy little bastard he was. So macho and full of himself. I picked out a bottle of red wine from the baker's rack in the corner, opened it and poured two glasses, silently shoving one across the counter towards the stove where he was standing. He took a swallow and smiled approvingly at me. At last I had done something right.

As he continued with his solitary preparation of the meal; making a salad of lettuce and onions, peering into the pan where the sausage sizzled and oozed reddish liquid, studiously ignoring the rice simmering in its pot, I sat back, sipped my wine and watched him silently. He was only thirty-three, but for some reason he didn't seem that much younger than me. Maybe because of his take-charge attitude and the way he dominated the kitchen. I had to admit that when he wasn't annoying me, I found him strangely intriguing.

"If you are Portuguese, where did you get the name Joe? Is that a Portuguese name?" I asked.

His eyes were wary as he turned to look at me. "That's what they call me in this country."

"But, what does your mother call you?" I was pleased at having thought of this way to find out his real name.

"My mother calls me Jose." His eyes were on my face again, watching and waiting.

"Jo-zeh" I tried to make it sound the way he did, letting the last syllable drop off lazily at the end. "In this country we would say, 'Ho-say," I said.

"That's Spanish - how they say it - not Portuguese." His lip curled disdainfully. He drew himself up straight and looked proudly at me.

"My name is Jose Manuel Barbosa da Costa. My grandmother, when she saw me when I was borned, she gived me Jose Manuel, and Barbosa was my mother's name. That's it. Jose Manuel Barbosa da Costa. But in this country, the mangia-cakes call me Joe . . . Joe Costa. That's all they can say of it. It makes them happy." He shrugged and turned back to his work.

"What do you mean, mangia-cakes? Who are these mangia-cakes?" I asked.

"Anglos . . .you know . . .anyone who's not Portuguese."

"Am I a mangia-cake?"

He hesitated for a moment watching me. "Yes."

"That's not very nice. Why do you say that?" The nervy little bugger was insulting me in my own house.

"You call us pork chops . . .we call you mangia-cakes. That's the way it is." He shrugged his shoulders and looked away.

I stared at him, trying to digest this information. "I have never called anyone a porkchop in my whole life," I said.

"Don't worry. We can laugh about it. Sometimes we call each other pork chops too." He said this apologetically. "One night I was in a bar near my house and this guy came in that I knew, and he sat down, and we had a few beers and he started singin' at me. He called me a pork chop in the singin' and I got mad and I singed back at him. After a while, we singed back and forth and then he goes like this with his hand and he gived up." Joe extended his hand toward this imaginary adversary, as though to shake hands, but the look on his face was combative . . . challenging.

"What do you mean . . . he singed at you?"

"He singed at me . . . that's the way it is in my country. Sometimes two guys will sit down and have a few drinks and they say this and that, and then, if they know how, they will sing at each other until one of them gives up. Then he puts out his hand and that tells the other guy that he gives up, so he wins"

My curiosity was aroused. "What does he win?"

"The singin'. He wins the singin'." Joe frowned. "It isn't easy. It has to be the right sound to it at the end. And the bounce . . . it has to bounce right. Some guys can do it but it's hard . . . not everyone can sing like that."

"How did you learn to sing like that?"

"My father - he was famous for singin' in my country. Sometimes two or three other guys would stand up with him but always he would be the last one standing. All the rest would shake his hand. They couldn't look in his eyes. I guess I learned it from my dad."

I was truly lost now. "I still don't quite understand what you mean. Could you sing at me?" I said.

"No . . . no. I couldn't do that with you." He thought for a moment, then turned back to poke at the sausage in the pan. "No, it's too hard in English. It doesn't work."

"Then do it in Portuguese . . . please . . . I just want to hear what it sounds like."

The frown on his face reflected his mental effort as he thought about it, then suddenly he looked at me and began to sing. His voice was deep and pleasant.

Tu es uma linda Mulher
 Ninguem me diga que nao
Seja o que Deus quiser
Hoje ontem e amanha

I listened in amazement. "What did you say? Did you insult me?" I smiled at him to let him know that it was alright, encouraging him to tell me what he had said. He looked steadily into my eyes and repeated the phrases in English:

You are a beautiful womans
No one can tell me that you are not.
Let it be what God wants
Today, yesterday and tomorrow.

I felt my cheeks burning with the intensity of his words and the ardent admiration in his smoky gaze. Had he really made this up for me? What was the matter with him? My God, he was talking to me like a lover. The silence in the kitchen was broken only by the sound of his breathing. His eyes continued to bore into mine, unblinking.

I busied my hands with my wine glass, trying to recover my composure. Why was he here? What did he want with me?

"Do you have any salt?" he asked.

"What?" I said. I was in some sort of a daze . . . my brain totally disconnected from the words he was saying.

"Salt . . . I need some salt for the rice."

With an effort I pulled myself together. "Yes, right there on the top of the stove," I said, as he shook salt liberally into the pot of rice. I watched in growing alarm. On and on, the shaker moved up and down until I couldn't stand it any longer.

"Stop." The shrill sound of my voice startled both of us.

"What's the matter with you? Don't you know that the rice needs salt?" He sounded puzzled.

"Yes, but not so much. Please. My blood pressure will be through the roof."

"Okay." Reluctantly he set the shaker down on the counter, but not before he had given it a few more shakes to let me know he was still in charge.

"Do you have any pepper?" Laughter started up again in my throat. He was impossible. I had never met anyone like him before. One minute he was reciting love poetry and the next he was looking for the pepper sitting right under his nose.

"It's there on the top of the stove." *Right beside the salt, you stupid Porkchop!*

Shake, shake, shake.

"This is not pepper. It's black. Pepper is red." Now he looked wounded, as though I had deliberately misled him, trying to sabotage his precious untouchable rice.

What the hell did he want? "What kind of pepper? Chili pepper?" I asked.

"No, red pepper. Like this, but it's red."

"Paprika? Do you mean paprika?" He was really starting to piss me off.

"Show me." His eyes narrowed suspiciously.

I pushed him aside roughly and opened the cupboard above his head, revealing the spices neatly arranged in their rack. When he saw the paprika his face broke into a smile.

"Yes, that's it . . . pepper," he exclaimed, beginning to shake it into the pot. Once, twice, then . . . "Oh, that's enough."

I couldn't believe him ... a ton of salt and two shakes of paprika. With my hand over my mouth I muffled the sound which was bubbling uncontrollably up from my mid-section. It felt strange. I hadn't laughed like that for years.

He took no notice of me but went on with his preparations, flip-flops slapping on the hardwood floor as he moved stolidly from the salad to the sausage sputtering noisily in the fat. His nostrils flared occasionally to fully capture the pungent aroma as he spoke with sensuous anticipation of the experience to come.

"You never tasted anything like this. You are going to *lurve* it."

I struggled to maintain my composure. I poured another glass of wine. What in God's name had this crazy little man done to me? He seemed to have me completely under his spell. "It will be ready soon," he announced. His tone was reverent, charged with the importance of the occasion. "Do you have any plates?"

To my surprise dinner was delicious. He really did know what he was doing. The rice was white and fluffy, the salad of lettuce and onions simply dressed with olive oil and vinegar, crisp and refreshing, and the *pièce de résistance,* Momma's sausage, a pungent and mouth-watering treat. We ate for the most part in silence. Jose obviously believed that taking nourishment was a serious business not to be detracted from by idle chitchat. He filled the wine glasses for each of us and refilled them when they were close to being empty. Grunts of encouragement from him accompanied my first taste of the sausage and he smiled when he could see that I liked it. Opening the casing of his sausage with his fork he retrieved a bit of the tender part near the end and held it out for me, nodding his head as he urged me to eat more of the rich meat. Obediently, I opened my mouth.

"You see. I told you my mother makes the best sausage. I was right . . . yes?"

"You were right . . . yes. It's good." I was really enjoying the unusual flavour of the tasty meat. He raised his wine glass with a great show of ceremony and tipped it toward me, indicating that I should do the same.

"A nós." His gaze was warm and familiar. "To us."

"To us," I repeated as our glasses touched briefly. I wondered how we had so suddenly become a pair. Perhaps it was the sharing of wine and the good food or maybe it was the low light from the fixture that hung over the table in the kitchen enclosing us in a circle of intimacy. The gold-flecked eyes of this man, Jose, locked onto my face and stared without blinking into my eyes, seeming to probe beyond their depths, looking perhaps for a place to breach the wall I had so carefully constructed to protect my heart.

"You have beautiful eyes." His voice was gentle and persuasive. "Can you see in the dark with those eyes?" I was surprised by the sincerity of his expression. I caught my breath and held it. Then abruptly his explosive laugh defused the intensity of the moment.

Embarrassed, I deftly turned Jose's words against him.

Moments on a Staircase

"Yes, I can see in the dark, and I also know when I look at someone if they are telling the truth or if they are trying to con me." I said, staring at him coldly. How stupid did he think I was?

His chin lifted proudly. "Why do you say this? I am not here to *explore* you. Is that what you think? That I bring sausages for you from my mother's kitchen and cook for you so that I can *explore* you? I guess I should go now if that is what you think." He made an exaggerated move to push himself back from the table and get up from his chair. I had to smile at the melodramatic way in which he was getting ready to make his exit.

But then I began to feel sorry that I had perhaps really hurt him by reacting so callously to his compliment. Why couldn't I just accept it when someone said something nice about me? Why did I always have to spoil things?

"Oh, please don't be mad, Jose. I really appreciate what you did tonight. You're a wonderful cook. I was just kidding you . . . teasing, do you understand? I'm sorry." I reached out to touch his hand where it rested on the table.

He sat back in his chair once again and lifted the half-empty bottle of wine, obviously willing to forgive me, although he retained a shadow of his injured feelings in the hurt expression that lingered around his eyes. "You are too much," he said as he filled the glasses and tipped his towards me, ducking his head in salutation. *"A nós."*

"A no-suh." My pronunciation matched his more easily this time. I took a sip and realized that I'd drank a lot of wine. It had slipped down warmly making me feel relaxed and daring. This was certainly the most interesting evening I'd had in a long time. I was glad he hadn't left. My cheeks were flushed and pink from his flattering words as well as from the wine, and I was beginning to enjoy the contest of wits with him. I hadn't played the game since Paul's death. I realized how much I'd missed it, the back and forth steps of that ancient dance of man and woman. The beat of it and the bending. The fire of excitement in the playing.

Now this young man, so exotic and different from what I knew seemed to be challenging me to take up the sport once again. But how could this be? He was so much younger than I was.

"Do you have a deck of cards?" Jose's voice brought me back to the present.

"Sure." I got the bridge decks from the table in the hallway and put them in front of him. What on earth was he up to now? I wondered.

"I will teach you to play *bijca da dez*," he said. It was a simple game of following suit and trying to amass the most points, with tens having the highest value. Face cards counted too, and Jose insisted that kings beat aces and jacks were higher than queens. I was confused but attempted to figure it out as I lost several games. I watched with amusement as he peered surreptitiously at the bottom card while he was dealing, making sure, if it was one that counted big that it ended up in his pile. As he manipulated the cards deftly with his large hands, I noticed that the skin of the right one had been crudely marked with five small blue circles in a domino pattern on the fleshy part between thumb and forefinger.

"What's that for?" I pointed to the marks.

"That's for my country." He stopped and looked at his hand. "It's the emblem for Portugal. I did it with a blue pen. Ooooh, it hurt a lot. Some people thinks that's for the number of years in jail but I haven't been in jail, only for one night. Me and my friends went to this bar and we drinked up a storm and I got in a fight with this guy and the bouncer threw us all out. We didn't want to go, so we tried to fight with him but the owner called the cops. My friends ran away fast and jumped over the fence, but I climbed a tree. I wasn't tall enough to get over that fence. When the cops came they shined the light up at me and made me comed down and they taked me to jail . . . but just for one night. We were all *lorded* that night but I was the only one who got caught because I had to go and climb that tree instead of getting away over the fence."

I tried not to show the astonishment I felt. He had just given me a glimpse of the tough little streetwise character he really was. I decided to ignore the bar room brawl and focus on the mention of his size.

"Are all the people in your family small?" It seemed rude but I felt the conventional rules of polite conversation had been breached long ago.

"No. My mother is little, but my father is taller than me and my brothers are too. I was the first one to comed out and my mother says I made room in her stomach for the other ones to grow bigger." Then a cunning look came over his face. "Not all of me is small though." Once again laughter erupted from him, this time accompanied by a suggestive look at his crotch.

Oh God, here he goes again, I thought. One minute I felt empathy for him and the next revulsion. I ignored his suggestive remark, trying to assume a dignified, schoolteacher attitude, hoping it would bring the conversation back to a more civilized level.

"You are not so tall, but you are strong." I said, not wanting to hurt his feelings again. And, after all it was true. For the past two weeks I had watched the landscaping crews hoist the damp thirty-pound rolls of sod onto their shoulders and carry them wherever they were needed. Hour after hour they went about their back-breaking work, raking and grading the long expanses of earth around the new condos, laying the unwieldy rolls of grass and stamping the edges with their heavy boots. A horde of anonymous worker bees swarming over the landscape day after day. Faceless...until now.

I got up from my chair and picked out another bottle of wine from the rack. If opened it and reached over his shoulder to refill Jose's empty glass. My breasts pressed lightly into his shoulder as I bent over him and I felt his warmth and strength radiate through the thin material of my shirt. Before I knew what was happening, he was on his feet with his arms around my waist, squeezing until I felt my spine might crack. Instinctively, I pushed against his chest, trying to escape from his crushing hold.

Oh God, this was it. He was going to kill me now.

"I am strong, neh? I could lift you up with these arms and put you on my shoulder," he said. To my horror, he seemed about to prove his prowess.

"You are hurting me," I protested loudly. The pressure of his arms decreased a little. Still he held me fast in his embrace. Then he threw his head back, laughing aloud, a kind of fiendish sound, and began to move with me in tow as though we were dancing.

"Can you do the lambada?" He didn't wait for a reply but tucked one of his legs between mine so I was cradled on his hip. As he began to rotate his torso, I could feel the hardness of his groin bumping suggestively against my thighs. He began to sing in his native tongue, a kind of Latin sounding song. His lips were near my ear and the air from his laboured breathing ruffled the hair around the side of my face as we moved together in this bizarre dance with him doing all the work, almost lifting me off my feet as we swooped and turned this way and that. I was carried easily along with him, nestled against his side like some overgrown baby, too dizzy and bewildered to protest.

And then something amazing happened to me. I began to catch fire from him and enjoy the whole thing, the closeness, the roughness of his beard against my cheek, the obvious strength of the arms that imprisoned me. If these were my final moments on earth, I decided I was going to fully experience them. I put my head back and laughed, a wild sound. Around and around the kitchen we whirled, bumping into the walls, unseating the pictures that hung there, setting the dishes on the baker's rack precariously in motion. By now he was humming, running out of breath and I was panting from the effort of trying to keep up with his savage movements. Out the doorway of the kitchen we gyrated and into the living room where we lurched around the coffee table several times before he slowed down at last and deposited me on the sofa, He fell beside me, laughing and coughing.

I lay still, heart pounding, trying to catch my breath. My mind was reeling, and I felt faint. and totally helpless. Obviously, he could do whatever he wanted with me. I was not capable of getting away from him. He had destroyed all my defenses. Even my glib tongue couldn't save me.

I started to laugh when I realized what a ludicrous picture I must make, lying on my back on the sofa, knees bent over the edge, arms splayed out, bosom heaving, like some ancient porn star after a stormy session on the couch. And Jose wasn't much better. His face was red from his efforts and sweat stood out on his forehead. The shiny black hair was falling into his eyes as he leaned back helplessly against one of the cushions at the end of the sofa. We looked at each other and laughter rocked both of us for several moments. What a pair we made. Old and young, short and tall, worlds apart culturally and economically and yet joined in one hilarious moment in time. He moved toward me then and slipped his arm under my shoulders. The laughter stopped.

I turned to look into his eyes, so close, so dark, burning into mine. I felt the heat from him warming the space between our bodies as he leaned towards me. Oh God! He was going to kiss me

. His lips gently brushed my mouth, pressing softly. I couldn't resist looking at him. His eyes were closed and the handsome face at close range excited me - so smooth and unlined with a new growth of dark hair already making a shadow where his beard should be. Long dark lashes masked his eyes. Was he peeking back at me? I thought I saw a glint of light beneath the lowered lids. I decided to close my eyes too and enjoy the sensations sweeping through me. Something told me not to look - just to seize the moment and allow myself to feel the long-suppressed life welling up inside. He seemed to sense the relaxing of the final barriers between us as he turned his body into mine, claiming my mouth more forcefully now, breath coming noisily through his nostrils. Obviously, he wanted more. He was kissing me with purpose, with desire, putting his whole body into it, seducing me.

I arched my back and leaned toward him, aching for the touch that I had been missing for so long. He met me full on, adjusting his arms to envelope my upper body, cradling my breasts against the hard contours of his chest. And all the while the kiss continued. He moved his head back and forth, slowly insinuating his tongue between my lips, thrusting it suggestively against the insides of my cheeks. I could feel it all the way to my toes. My hips began a subtle involuntary rocking, moving my lower body closer and closer to him, as I sought a release from the powerful feelings that surged through me. I could hear little moans coming from deep in my throat, but I made no effort to stifle them. It felt great to let go. Long ago Paul had made me feel this way, perhaps too long ago. But no, my body remembered, and I was kissing Jose back, working my tongue around the corners of his mouth, promising him the world with the movement of my hips against his leg. Jose pulled himself up and away from me. His eyes were half-closed as he looked at me.

"I think we should go to your bed now." His voice had a ragged, urgent sound as he stood up. "You go and get ready; I will meet you there." Then, glancing at the closed doors along the main hallway of the condo he smiled ruefully. "Which one is your bedroom?"

"In there." I pointed to the door at the end of the hall and walked in a kind of daze to the bathroom. Closing the door carefully I turned on the light and looked at myself in the large mirror over the marble vanity. What a sight I was. My cheeks were flushed and pink with wine and excitement. My lips looked puffy and the lipstick had been rubbed off leaving my mouth with a slightly bruised appearance. The eyes that he had admired were truly glowing now.

I smiled, wondering what it was I was supposed to do. "Get ready," he had said. But how was I supposed to do that? Have a bath? Comb my hair? What did he expect? And why just me? Why wasn't he getting ready? Didn't he even have to wash his hands?

I leaned on the sink peering closely into the mirror. What was the matter with me? I hadn't had sex for two years and now there was a good-looking guy in bed waiting for me. But wasn't it dangerous? What about safe sex? Would he have a condom? I remembered the rainbow- coloured ones that the bridge club girls had given me as a joke before I went to Greece. I turned on the tap so he wouldn't hear me rummaging through the drawers of the vanity. The little foil packages of Trojans were still in my travel case and I slipped one into the pocket of my jeans.

Oh shit! After all that wine I had to pee. But my muscles were so tight that only a dribble came out. I washed my hands, squeezed some toothpaste onto one finger and rubbed it around inside my mouth then spit it out and rinsed the sink with the running water. Hopefully he would hear it and envision me rinsing myself off, like he had done with the pots in the kitchen. A mist of perfume from the tray on the counter completed my preparations.

Taking a deep breath I opened the bathroom door and suddenly giddy with wine and anticipation, headed unsteadily down the hall to the bedroom.

In the doorway of the darkened room I hesitated. I sensed his presence but didn't know where he was. In a few moments my eyes became accustomed to the low light and I could make out the pale outline of his body on top of the satin duvet, naked except for his socks. He was leaning back on the cushions, arms spread out, eyes closed, like a sacrificial lamb lying quiet and resigned on the altar.

Jose on the cross.

Panic stirred the wine in my stomach. The feelings he had aroused in me were still strongly pulsating throughout my body, but he looked so young and vulnerable lying there. I paused at the side of the bed. I didn't think I could go through with it now.

Then he opened his eyes.

"Hurry up, it's cold in here. My *ting* is shrinking." Jose laughed and patted the bed, inviting me to join him.

Moments on a Staircase

My mind was racing. I thought of Paul, no longer able to feel what I was feeling. I remembered the horror of that day in the basement of the hospital when they left me alone to say goodbye to his lifeless body. The dead eyes that looked up at me had been glittering empty sapphires, robbed forever of their sensibility. I decided not to think. One minute you were alive with all your senses working, and the next minute it was all over - forever. Somehow Paul seemed to be trying to tell me to live while I had the chance. It should be the most natural thing in the world, to eat and dance, to laugh and make love, that's the way life ought to be. It didn't matter to Jose that I was old enough to be his mother. For some reason he wanted me. What could be simpler than that? No games, no grudges, no pretense, just fulfillment of an urgent desire, a passionate encounter that would exist only for that one moment and then be gone, giving me something to remember in my old age. What harm could it do?

Slowly, I unbuttoned my blouse and let the smooth silk slide from my shoulders. I could feel a joyous freedom surging up through my whole body. At last I stood half naked before him, reveling in the power I felt as he watched me undress, passion glowing from his dark eyes. It had been so long...so long since a man had looked at me that way. I took the condom out of my pocket and held it in my teeth, like a rose. Then I wiggled out of my jeans and pulled off my underpants with a flourish, tossing them into the corner of the room. One of my knees was on the bed now, and then the other as I crawled slowly towards Jose, homing in on the heat of his body, searching for the refuge of his desire for me.

****

A few hours later he was gone and once more I found herself staring at my image in the bathroom mirror. I felt like someone else, but the face that stared back at me didn't look that different. Except that my eyes were still glowing, pale green and lustrous in an other-worldly sort of way. I remembered how Jose had stared at them in the dim light of my bedroom.

"Can you see in the dark with those eyes?" he had asked again. He seemed genuinely afraid of them.

"Yes, I can see right through you." Once more I enjoyed my little joke at his expense. But as I gazed at my reflection my expression changed. *Oh God, I'd just had sex with a man half my age!*

The laughter that welled up in me began to take on an air of hysteria. How could I have done it? And, how could he? I leaned closer to the glass, my finger tracing the little lines beside my eyes and around my mouth. I wondered if he had noticed them. Then I remembered the darkness and was relieved. But how did I feel to him.... all soft and mushy? My cheeks burned with the shame of it. I remembered Jose lying silently beside me, on his back, arms outstretched, eyes closed. He was probably trying to think of someone else, someone young and beautiful. At last he had moved one of his hands to touch my breast, fondle it, give it a squeeze or two, like milking one of his goats, I imagined.

I laughed as I recalled how he lay there, so silently, waiting for me to make all the moves, almost afraid to touch me until suddenly, to my amazement, he had muttered through clenched teeth, "I am coming."

But then, the tears turned sour in my throat and just as suddenly as the laughter had begun, it turned to racking sobs that squeezed my ribs in a vise grip. I thought of the picture of Paul hanging beside the bed, of those blue eyes, captured in a moment of liveliness, staring at me, forced to watch silent and powerless as I wallowed in bed with this young stranger. I reached blindly for a towel from the rack nearby and buried my face in it as I slowly slumped to the floor. I hadn't cried like this for two years. After a few minutes, when the tears abated somewhat, I remembered Paul making love to me, his patient hands caressing me and bringing me to life. Fresh rivers of sadness washed my cheeks. The tears melted away the guilt and some of the anger I'd amassed as armor for my emptiness since he left me.

After a while I slowly composed myself. The towel dropped from my hands exposing the raw and ugly truth in the mirror. I was old. No one would ever love me like that again. And certainly it would not be that enterprising little impostor who had just a few minutes ago gone out my front door.

"I will hold you in my eyes until I see you again," he had whispered as he left, reaching up to brush his lips against the corner of my mouth. No wonder I hadn't been able to resist him. Is that what Vasco da Gama said to the Queen of Spain before he sailed off to conquer the world, his pockets crammed with her golden doubloons?

The punch line of an old joke flashed into my head. Now that we know what you are, we just have to settle on a price. I guessed my price was a Portuguese sausage. If he brought me two more sausages, would that be like having the banns read in church? My God, we'd be engaged!

Guess what, kids? Momma's gonna get married. Here's your new Daddy. His name is Jose. He's almost your age, so you can all have fun and play together.

I shook my head vigorously to dispel the image I had conjured up, tried to convince myself to get over it. The whole sordid affair was, after all, just one crazy moment in a lifetime of duty and moral uprightness. Surely a person was allowed an error of judgement one time. And the whole experience could be beneficial as far as my writing was concerned. I had come closer to finding out how Jocasta might have felt in the arms of her young lover. The best thing though, was that no one had been hurt. I had survived, and as for Jose, he was probably sitting in a pub somewhere, amusing his porkchop friends with the story of the free wine and the raunchy old mangia-cake he had just nailed.

As I hung up the towel and turned off the bathroom light, I made up my mind to forget the whole thing and forgive myself. Sometimes the longing to feel loved, to be in a man's arms was more than I could bear, and I had simply seized the day, as my friends were always telling me to do. When I cleaned it up a bit and told the girls the story at bridge club, they would get a kick out of my amorous adventure. No good shocking the shit out of them, though. I would tell them he was fifty, not thirty-three.

But somewhere deep down inside, a faint thought was struggling to life in my brain. As he had touched me, it was as though some of his strength and vitality had flowed into me, reversing the tide of age and tears, making me whole again. Somehow this brief and awkward encounter had mended some of my ragged bits and, improbable as it seemed, I found myself hoping I would see him again.

Chapter 16 - A Christmas Letter

Dear Loved Ones,

This is our tenth Christmas without Paul. I know we each miss him and wish he could be here with us. He really loved Christmas; the turkey dinner (remember the year he sliced his hand with the electric knife and had to go to emergency?), the pudding with the hard sauce (he had to make it because it was so hard to stir), singing carols at the dining room table, (Paul's nice tenor voice chimed in with harmony on all the old familiar tunes), watching the kids open their gifts (one year we just got a saddle on Johnny West's horse before the sun came up!), parking the brand new snowmobile with the big red bow on it at the end of the sidewalk and watching the boys' faces light up with amazement when they saw it, then gritting his teeth when they ran it into a tree later on that day. Nothing was ever allowed to spoil Christmas, though!

He always watched Alistair Sim's version of *A Christmas Carol* and every year, when Bob Cratchit comes home from the graveyard where Tiny Tim is buried and says to his wife, "I think he is very content, my dear. Oh Tim, my Tiny Tim!" I would sneak a peek at Paul through my own tears and he would be crying, too. What a softie he was. For forty-two Christmases he was there with us, usually in the background, doing his thing, but loving every minute of it and loving each one of you.

For a long time now, I have searched for a way to say how I feel after being without him for ten Christmases. I looked in all my anthologies of poetry with the beautiful words written by famous poets about the loss of a loved one and nothing seemed to fit. Then, today, Christmas Eve, 2010, I read some letters to God written by children from all over the world and reported in the *Hamilton Spectator*. I have paraphrased the one I liked best and I want to share it with you because it tells exactly how I feel.

Dear Paul,

I am trying to accept who I am without you. But I miss you so much I don't know which of us is gone.

Yours forever, Mary

Chapter 17 - Better Late Than Never

When my eightieth birthday was looming large on the horizon of my life, I won my first and only prize for writing.

"Congratulations!" the e-mail began enthusiastically. "You have won the Hamilton Short Works Redeemer College Award for your Off the Radar Unpublished Story, *'My Theatrical Career'*. A cash award will be presented to you at the Hamilton Public Library on November 18, 2018. Details will follow."

I was taken by surprise. I hardly remembered entering the contest several months before. A friend had encouraged me to do so, and for a brief moment I wondered if he was playing some kind of a joke on me. The story didn't seem prize-worthy to me; a small reminiscence of my first job at the Fox Theatre in Stoney Creek. I was thirteen at the time. How could this little story have miraculously acquired historic importance when it happened such a short while ago? But when I really thought about it, it was sixty-seven years ago. Sixty-seven years! How could that be?

I remembered that job at the Fox with vivid clarity, even though the world has gone through the atomic bomb scare of the fifties, the assassination of JFK, the Korean War, the Vietnam War and other significant events. Somehow, the stories of my life were now ancient treasures like the Dead Sea Scrolls. Who knew?

I have always loved to write--loved the sound of my own voice in print. My first story was about a paper maché animal I had made in grade seven. I called him Murgatroyd Mudhole. He followed me home one day and became my constant companion. I fed him out of a little bowl in the kitchen and took him for walks with a rope tied around his neck. He would clump around the house with me and sleep on my bed at night. I wrote adventures for him and left them where my mother could find them. I hoped she would feel guilty because her irrational fear of animals had made it impossible for us to have a real pet. Mother said she liked the stories very much, but it didn't change her mind. Our house remained petless.

But I enjoyed the experience of creating a world of my own where no one could interfere. I was the author, and as such, had total control of everything that happened. It was a heady feeling, one that I continued to amuse myself with all my life. From my Murgatroyd stories, I graduated to humorous letters for my friends and relatives and occasional poems for special events in my life.

"Murray is retiring," my friends would say. "Write a poem for him." And I did.

Through the years I enjoyed making people laugh, and if my literary efforts were sometimes less than stellar, my friends didn't let me know. After all, they loved me anyway.

"This is great!" they'd say. "You are a terrific writer."

Encouraged by their admiration, I wrote some little stories about special events in my usually uneventful life and entered one of them in a contest for unpublished authors. Eureka! A group of total strangers bestowed on my little story an award which consisted of some cash and an official looking document on the stationery of David Christopherson, MP It was enclosed in a green, faux leather folder embossed with gold letters proclaiming, House of Commons, Canada.

I was so amazed by this unexpected honour, that I told no one. I went to the ceremony at the Hamilton Public Library by myself. I hadn't visited the downtown branch for a number of years and at first, I wasn't sure I was in the right place. Was this a library? Rows of computers filled the large open space as I entered through the front doors. The stations were occupied by people peering at the screens in the glow of the internet There were no books anywhere to be seen.

Straight ahead was a small desk manned by a friendly person who directed me past shelves of discs, to a large back room. I entered the door marked McNab Room as I had been instructed to do.

On a stage, musicians were setting up music stands and chairs to form a kind of orchestra. To the left of the orchestra was a microphone on a stand next to a wooden podium. Several people were milling about near the steps leading up to the stage.

Chairs arranged in rows in a semi-circle filled the room. Most of the seats were already occupied by young people. I quickly ascertained that I was the oldest person in the room. I saw a single chair on the far side of the room in the middle of the third row from the front. It was as far away from the steps up to the stage as one could get.

"Excuse me. Pardon me," I said, as I barged my way to the empty chair, stepping on feet and nearly falling into several laps on the way.

Moments on a Staircase

On my chair I found a programme announcing that several amateur musical groups were to entertain the crowd before the presentations began. There were eight different categories of stories. Prizes were to be awarded and each winner was given five minutes to read a bit of their story. A Rastafarian minister opened the proceedings with a sort of incantation to the gods of ganga and reggae. One of the musical groups played for a bit, some unrecognizable tune that went on at length.

I could see that it was going to be a long afternoon. My name appeared near the end of the program in a strange category called "Off the Radar Un-Published Non-Fiction".

I settled in for an interminable wait. It was then that I felt the unmistakeable urge to pee.

I couldn't go back on that impossible route past all those people to get to the washroom, so I gritted my teeth, determined to hang on. After all, how long could this take?

It seemed to take forever. One after another, bright-eyed young folks skipped up the steps to the microphone and read excerpts from their winning works. Angst-ridden, gloomy, heart-wrenching stories torn from the tatters of their young lives. Lives which I observed had hardly even begun.

"Wait till you're pushing eighty," I muttered to myself.

Meanwhile the urge to piddle became stronger and stronger. I tightened muscles I didn't think I had anymore and prayed it would soon be my turn. And finally, it was.

"Mary Haylock," intoned the master of ceremonies solemnly. "Winner of the Off the Radar Unpublished Non-Fiction Award for her story, 'My Theatrical Life'".

Moments on a Staircase

I rose from my chair very slowly because my leg muscles had atrophied during the long wait. As I gained my feet at last, the papers I had been holding in my lap slid to the floor scattering in disarray under the chairs and feet of the folks in the row ahead of me. A kind man sitting next to me gathered them up and thrust them into my hands as my purse slipped from my shoulder and hit him on the head.

"Thank-you. Sorry," I mumbled as I began the long sideways trek out to the end of the aisle. People pulled in their feet and pressed themselves back into the safety of their seats as I bumbled by.

"Excuse me...sorry," I muttered.

Finally I reached the end of the row and headed across the enormous room in front of the stage. I walked very slowly, hoping I would not fall over. After what seemed like an eternity, I had made it only halfway across. There was dead silence in the room. All eyes were following my laborious trip to the stairs. In order to break the tension, I turned to smile at the audience.

"Have faith," I said. "I will make it eventually."

My attempt at humour was met with more silence. I knew I was in big trouble. I kept moving and finally reached the steps up to the stage. To my horror, there was no handrail in sight. I hesitated at the bottom step. Should I attempt it? I was feeling slightly dizzy from my long trek and it occurred to me I hadn't eaten any lunch that day. Not good when you're pre-diabetic. I felt like Marie Antoinette at the steps to the guillotine. I can only imagine the terrified look I must have had on my face.

At this moment, one of the men on the stage came down and took my hand. With the help of this good Samaritan I made it up to the top and staggered to the lectern. I held on with both hands, puffing hard and trying to get my breath. With horror, I realised that I felt a sneeze coming on. I grabbed my nose and managed to somehow smother it.

One of the people standing nearby stepped forward and extended his hand. I shook it as he presented me with a green folder. I have no idea who he was.

"Congratulations, Mrs. Haylock" he said. "Would you now favour us with a reading of your prize-winning story?"

I shuffled through my papers and found the story. I think I read it, but I'm not really sure. I heard myself speaking in a kind of emotionless monotone. My mouth was so dry that my tongue kept clicking off my front teeth. When I was through, I looked up from my paper at the faces of the audience. No one laughed. No one was smiling. There was only silence. I stared dumbly at them and they stared blankly back.

It had been my intention to thank all the people in my life who had guided me to this auspicious culmination of my literary career. Like the winner of an Oscar, I had pictured myself bowing and smiling into the camera as the crowd roared their approval.

Instead, the master of ceremonies clapped and this started a small ripple of polite applause as I grabbed my folder and bolted down the stairs. This time, I walked across the room in front of the stage without anyone noticing. They were gathering up their things and leaving. So was the orchestra and the organizers of the event. No one spoke to me as I scurried out the door clutching my award.

I fled into the fresh afternoon air outside the library where I flagged down a passing taxi. The driver was a friendly fellow named Aymen. I took this to be an omen of some kind. As I opened my green folder to have a closer look at the words inscribed there, a plain white envelope slid out and fell into my lap. Inside were two crisp, new bills. One hundred-and fifty-dollars. My first and only monetary gain from my years of writing. I smiled as my heart filled with a warm glow of pride. I was now an author, for sure.

What do you do? folks will say to me.

I am a writer, I will say proudly.

I tipped Aymen fifty. It's what Margaret Atwood would do, I thought. A magnanimous gesture from a successful author.

Chapter 18 - The End

Last night I dreamt I went to Manderley again. Oh, no. Wait a minute. That's such a perfect first line, I felt compelled to borrow it. I'm sure Daphne DuMaurier wouldn't mind. But that would be plagiarism, so I won't. Well, maybe just a bit of it. Let me start again.

Last night I dreamt I died and went to Heaven, peacefully in my sleep, just the way I had always hoped I would. I didn't really want to go, but if I did have to go, that was a good way to go. It didn't hurt a bit. I just sort of floated up and up until I found myself in a pleasant place full of smiling people, some of whom I recognized at once.

There was my Bubba, sitting on a bench in the shade of a tree, his cane beside him, his wooden leg stretched out straight in front of him, just the way it was most comfortable for him.

When I was a baby, he let me sit on the bed where he lay dying and play with the shiny screws that held his leg together. Bubba had lost that leg many years before in an accident at the sawmill in Ailsa Craig, owned by his father.. He was only nineteen years old when a workman fell onto the belt leading to the huge circular saw that ripped the logs into planks. As the helpless man got closer to the whirling blade, Bubba pushed the big lever to stop it. But he quickly saw that the blade would not stop turning in time to save the man. So he stuck his leg into the gears of the machine and it ground to an immediate halt. It also ground up Bubba's leg.

He managed quite well for the rest of his life with a wooden one, although at one time, he felt a pain in the missing limb and asked that it be dug up from its burial place and put into a larger container. After this, he was quite comfortable. He managed to father nine children, so it didn't appear to have bothered him that much. My father was the second youngest. He weighed twelve pounds when he was born, and they say grandma could be heard yelling all over town on the day he arrived.

"What's that ungodly noise?" the villagers asked.

"Oh, it's just Mrs. Gillies having another baby," someone replied. And they all went on about their day.

Grandma needed help with her brood, so Bubba hired a serving girl named Jen to look after the kids. Jen had a nickname for each child. Mildred was Mid, Edith was Dede, Muriel was Mornie, Rhoda was Dodie, Roy was Ted, Arthur, my dad, was Sam, and the baby, Gordon, was just...the baby. If you're counting, several of the earlier babies were, unhappily, stillborn.

As Bubba sat peacefully dreaming in the shade, I saw grandma approach and sit down next to him. He took her hand and smiled at her.

"Do you want to go for a nap?" he asked with a sly wink.

"No, Sam. Let's play gin rummy instead," she said, producing a deck of cards from her apron pocket.

"It's Sunday, Allie," he said. "You know we don't play cards on Sunday."

"Land sakes," grandma said. "I almost forgot. It seems like everyday is Sunday up here."

I felt my heart swell with a long ago love for them.

As I floated along on the gentle current of warm air that seemed to be holding me up, I saw a line of people patiently waiting to enter a large building. The doors were made of gold and the turrets and battlements were shining with a pearlescent glow in the sunshine. I saw my mother and father near the beginning of the line and I swooped down to where they were. They seemed much younger than I last remembered them and they were holding hands and obviously very much in love. I had to interrupt their loving looks at one another to get their attention.

"Hi," I said. "Remember me?"

"Of course," my mother said. "How could we forget you? Our first baby girl."

"Fatstuff," my father said, fondly, calling me by the pet name he had coined for me when I was a baby. "It's good to see you up here. Sometimes we wondered if you'd make it."

"I've missed you both very much," I said.

"We missed you too, honey," mother said. "So glad you're here now, with us again. Donnie's somewhere in this crowd. Have a look around. He'll be glad to see you, too."

"Why are you lined up to go in there?" I said, pointing at the large building.

"To see the show, of course," my mother said. "You'd better get in line soon, or you won't get in. It'll be a good show, I'm sure."

"What's it about?" I asked.

Moments on a Staircase

"You ought to know," my father said. He and mother looked at each other and laughed. "After all, it's all about you."

I floated on, slightly perplexed. All about me? Was I suddenly famous? Who would want to see a show about me, besides my parents, of course.

I noticed a little black dog frolicking about in the grass. It was Tippy. I'd know her anywhere. I picked her up and held her in my arms. She had been my loyal companion ever since Paul died. After his funeral, she slept on his pillow beside me. For three days, she refused to get out of bed or eat anything. I had to carry her outside.

After three days, she got up, shook herself off and went on about her job of looking after me. Enough of this sadness, she seemed to say. For thirteen years she was my little love. And then she got sick and became blind and one night she had trouble breathing. I took her to the vet in the middle of the night and he recommended she be put to sleep. She put her front legs around my neck and looked into my eyes, pleading with me to let her go on a bit longer, pain or no pain, but I nodded to let them know I was ready to let he go and they pushed the plunger on the intravenous needle inserted into her paw. She slumped in my arms, relaxing slowly into a deep sleep from which she never woke. I took her ashes home in my car in a box on the seat beside me. I remembered the awful feeling that I had betrayed her boundless trust in me.

But now, in this place, beyond earth, she seemed to have forgiven me. The look in her eyes was one of pure, unconditional love. I had let them kill her and still she adored me with every fibre of her being. How lucky I was to have experienced that kind of love in my lifetime.

Moments on a Staircase

I put her down on the grass and she took off, running wild and free in joyous circles, the way she used to do every day at four o'clock when she was a pup. "Having the crazies," we'd say as she zoomed around the house.

Suddenly the line started to move forward as people entered the beautiful building through the big crystal doors. I floated through and was ushered to a seat of honour in the first row of a large theatre that reminded me of The Fox, only *writ large*. I'm not sure, but I think it was Johnny Armondo who took me to my seat. He was older than I remembered, and handsome in a dark, exotic way. His uniform was white with golden embellishments, and he smelled wonderful, like roses and Old Spice after-shave.

As I sat down, I realized I was surrounded by other familiar faces, smiling at me. There was Mornie and Aunt Mid and Aunt Dede, sitting with their husbands. And Uncle Gord in his Airforce uniform from the Second World War, the one he was likely wearing on the day he died when his plane was shot down over the English Channel. He flipped me a salute and grinned.

My grandson, Jake, was right beside me and he reached out to hold my hand.

"Hello, Grandmama dearest," he said. "I have missed you very much."

"Me, too," I said. He looked so young and happy I could feel my heart about to burst with love for him.

"This should be a pretty good show, Grandmama, if I know you." He winked at me and gave my hand a squeeze. "Get comfy, cause they say it's quite long. My show was just a teaser. But this one has two acts. There's an intermission. I'll get you some orange pop and a mint patty then. What d'ya say?"

I didn't know what to say. I wondered again what this "show" everyone was talking about could possibly be. And why was it my show?

At this point celestial sounds arose from the orchestra pit, and I realized that harps and woodwinds were tuning up. The members of the orchestra rose to their feet as the conductor entered from the wings. He was a tall, shambling man, slightly stoop-shouldered, with long gangly arms and a mop of black hair flopping over his eyes. I recognized him immediately. It was My Donnie! He turned and bowed, then raised his head and looked directly at me. Our eyes met and I knew the smile that lit up his face was just for me. My Donnie still loved me.

Then he turned, climbed the podium and raised his baton as a hush fell over the audience. Everyone settled back in their seats.

A late arrival at the end of our row caused a slight stir. She slipped past the other patrons and ended up sitting on the other side of Jake. I had to look twice, but yes, it was Lou. Not the Lou in the Alzheimer's ward of Extenda-Care, slumped in her wheelchair and oblivious to the world. Lou, just the way I remembered her from our high school days: jet black curls bouncing around her tiny, porcelain face. A dainty Royal Doulton doll with a mischievous smile. She reached across Jake to touch my hand.

"Hi, Mare," she whispered, grinning at me with a twinkle in her eyes. "I hope they show some of our adventures. Remember Greece, and Italy and Fiji and Australia? I can hardly wait to see them all again." Then the show started. The overture began and the lights dimmed. I wondered if my show was to be a travelogue of our many trips together, as Lou hoped. I didn't have to wait long to find out.

Moments on a Staircase

The screen filled with a beautiful tableau of white clouds and cerulean skies full of birds soaring lazily in space, swooping and gliding gracefully through the air. Then the clouds changed shape and slowly began to form words. The words became, *"Moments on a Staircase, the Life and Times of Mary Haylock"*.

I sat very still but my mind was in high gear. What would this movie show? Just the good stuff, I hoped. Then I had a horrifying thought. What if it showed everything. That would really be a shocker for all these people that I loved. Surely, they wouldn't show absolutely everything. I started to think about some of the things I had done in my less-than-stellar career; the Greek bus driver, the Portuguese landscaper. Oh, my God! What would Paul think?

Paul. Where was he? Of all the people in my life, Paul was the one I most wanted to see. But I didn't want him to see everything I'd done since he died. He might not understand. I squirmed in my seat as I remembered some of them. I hadn't seen Paul anywhere. Maybe he didn't come to my show. I sank lower in my chair, trying to disappear as the credits rolled for my movie. And then I saw his name. Directed by Paul Haylock. He was the director of the thing. Surely, that meant he'd seen it and didn't disapprove too much. I hoped so. But, where was he?

It was then that I felt a warm breath on the back of my neck. Someone nuzzled my ear and I heard a familiar voice coming from the seat behind me.

"It's about time you got here, Mare," he said. "I've been waiting a long time for you."

I would know that voice anywhere. It was Paul. Suddenly I felt the hole in my heart begin to mend. Everything was alright now. I was back together the way I used to be, safe and whole. The feeling was indescribable. I knew that no matter what my movie revealed, the good and the bad, he was on my side, just like always. I turned to look at him, to see those blue eyes again, but he had left his seat and was on his way out.

"Wait, wait for me," I said. "Don't go without me. I have to ask you something. Did you really love me for all those years? You never said so. But did you love me?"

He stopped and turned around. "I bought you a horse, didn't I?" He was laughing as he walked away. Somehow, I knew I couldn't make him stay.

The movie started just then. The first scene was a city street, late at night. A blizzard filled the screen with swirling snow. The camera panned to show a large man shovelling madly. As he began to make some headway with the huge mounds of snow blanketing the driveway, an ancient, black sedan crept down the street and pulled into the cleared space. I saw Aunt Dodie in the back seat peeking out the window. She rolled down the glass and yelled at the man.

"Sorry it took so long, Art. The roads are impossible."

"Never mind," he said. "I'll go and get Eva. We've got to hurry."

Immediately I realized this was the story of the day I was born. It was the first one I had written for my memoir, *Moments on a Staircase*.

Is that what the show was going to be about? All the stories I had written about my life? And everyone would see them? The look on my face must have mirrored the growing anxiety in my stomach because Jake put an arm around me and gave my shoulder a squeeze.

"Don't worry, Grandmama," he said. "I did some pretty stupid things in my twenty-three years, but up here no one judges you.

Moments on a Staircase

You are your own judge. If you did bad stuff, you have to suffer watching the people you love see what you did. And same goes for the good stuff. It will make you happy to let them see that stuff. I think it's a pretty good idea and really the only fair way to treat people."

"Whose idea is it?" I asked.

Jake turned and pointed to a box on the upper tier of the theatre. It was ornately decorated and enclosed by a velvet curtain.

"He thought of it, I guess. After the Garden of Eden didn't work out so well, this seemed to be a fair way to punish folks for the bad stuff they do, and reward them for the good."

"Is *He* watching this movie now?" I looked over my shoulder at the resplendent box, hoping to catch a glimpse of the One inside.

"Likely. But He's seen it all before. Nothing surprises Him, so don't worry," Jake reassured me.

As my voice on the screen was heard reading the Burn's Day poem I had recited so many years before, a booming laugh came from behind the curtain. God has a sense of humour, I thought. Thank goodness.

At this moment I woke up. Reluctantly I came back to reality and realized it was all just a dream. I started to cry. I wanted to stay in that beautiful place with all the people I had once loved, who had loved me too. But I realized I couldn't. I would probably never see Manderley again.

Epilogue

The stories I have shared with you are true. Well, I may have put a bit of a shine on them here and there, just as I did on that dining room table long ago. But for the most part, they happened just the way I have told you. A few extraordinary moments in a long, ordinary life.

My next story is a bit of a mystery, however. Is it true or is it just the invention of an over-active imagination? I'll leave that up to you.

Moments on a Staircase

Nothing Lasts Forever

Late in the evening, an older man approaches the large, brick building. He pushes the numbers on the keypad outside and enters through the heavy front doors. He is short, slightly bent from years of hard work, broad in the shoulders with a thick chest and heavy legs. His dark hair is still thick, but shot with gray. He wears a black suit and shiny shoes that reflect the low lights in the dim foyer.

As he passes the elegant furniture arranged around a large marble fireplace, a place where no one ever sits, his gait is rolling, like a sailor keeping his balance on the deck of a ship at sea. In one of his large, square hands he carries a florist's box, long and white, with a red ribbon around it. When he reaches the nurses' station, the young attendant looks up from the book she is reading and smiles.

"Good evening, Mr. da Costa." She speaks softly so as not to disturb the quiet of the place now that everyone has settled for the night. "I think she is asleep."

A smile transforms his dark, somewhat sinister face. He is sixtyish, still quite handsome. He winks at the girl.

"She will wake up for me."

Moments on a Staircase

As he walks down the hall his nostrils flare with distaste. *These mangia-cakes smell bad when they get old,* he thinks.

When he reaches the last door, he opens it and sees her frail body curled up on the single bed, covered with a starchy white sheet. An overhead light glows on the wall, softly illuminating the picture of Jesus on the cross that hangs over the bed. The man touches her gently on the shoulder and she opens her eyes to see who has disturbed her sleep.

"Olá." He leans down close to her ear. "How are yew tonight?" His lips come together almost in a kiss. Her eyes open slowly and a smile softens her expression. She sees the box.

"What did yew bring me?" The voice that mimics him is cracked and dry from long, unbroken hours of silence.

He takes the ribbon off and opens it so she can see the long-stemmed, red roses nestled in their bed of white tissue paper. She looks, then pushes his gift aside with a fretful hand. Her sense of smell deserted her long ago. He puts the flowers on the night table and sits on the edge of the bed, raising her hand to press his lips against the papery skin. She fixes him with her pale eyes.

"Tell me the story," she murmurs.

With a sigh, he arranges the pillow and settles back beside her. Encircling her fragile shoulders with his strong arm, he pulls her against him. She closes her eyes as he begins, the words rumbling through his chest to her ear.

"*Um dia, eu vi uma linda mulher.*"

Her hands flutter in agitation on the top of the sheet, eyes open wide. "*Lindissima!*" she says.

"Okay, okay, *lindissima*." He begins again:

Moments on a Staircase

Um dia, eu vi uma lindissima mulher.
One day I saw a very beautiful woman.
Ela disse, 'Tu tens sede?' She said, "Are you thirsty?"
Eu disse, 'Eu bebo uma cerveja.' I said, 'I could drink a beer.'
Ela disse, 'okay'. She said, 'okay.'
Eu disse, 'Tu fodes?' I said, ' Do you fuck?'
Ela disse, 'Sim' She said, 'Yes.'

For a long moment they smile into each other's eyes; his, the colour of gasoline, eddying around his pupils in phosphorescent swirls. Hers, a milky green like a willow leaf floating on water. He feigns alarm at the sight of them:

"Can you see in the dark with those eyes?"

Tired of the game, she lies back on the pillow, waiting to drift back into the welcome nothingness of sleep. He takes her hand, kisses the scar that carves a thin white line across the blue veins of her wrist, holds it to his cheek, rubbing the delicate, transparent skin against his darkening beard. At the rough feel of his face she winces, pulling her hand away. With a sigh, she turns her face to the wall. Tenderly, he covers the slight curve of her thin shoulder with the blanket from the foot of the bed, tucking it gently into place with his large, calloused hands. As he opens the door to leave, her question trails after him, a faded whisper.

"Do you still love me, Jose?"

"Sometimes, deep down in my heart, I almost think I do."

She smiles as the door closes behind him.

Mary Haylock Bio:

Mary Haylock is a retired teacher with the Hamilton Board of Education, having spent 38 years working in the field of education. She graduated from McMaster University in Hamilton, Ontario in 1970 with a degree in English Literature.

Mary recently (Nov. 2018) won an award for a short story she entered in a contest sponsored by the Hamilton Arts and Letters magazine. Mary's first book, "9249*" was published in 2019. *"Moments on a Staircase"* published in 2020 is her second book.

www.ingramcontent.com/pod-product-compliance
Lightning Source LLC
Chambersburg PA
CBHW050355120526
44590CB00015B/1704